LITTLE HAWK
and the LONE WOLF

LITTLE HAWK
and the LONE WOLF

A MEMOIR

RAYMOND C. KAQUATOSH

WISCONSIN HISTORICAL SOCIETY PRESS

Published by the Wisconsin Historical Society Press
Publishers since 1855

© 2014 by the State Historical Society of Wisconsin
Paperback edition 2022

Publication of this book was made possible in part by a grant from the D. C. Everest
fellowship fund.

Printed in the United States of America
Cover design by Steve Biel
Cover illustration by steventhomasart.com
Interior design and typesetting by Mayfly Design

26 25 24 23 22   1 2 3 4 5

Library of Congress Cataloging-in-Publication Data is available for the hardcover
edition as follows:
Kaquatosh, Raymond C., 1924-
  Little Hawk and the Lone Wolf : a memoir / Raymond C. Kaquatosh.
    pages cm.
  ISBN 978-0-87020-650-4 (hardcover : alk. paper)—ISBN 978-0-87020-651-1
(e-book) 1. Kaquatosh, Raymond C., 1924- 2. Menominee Indians—Biography. 3. Menominee Indians—Social life and customs. 4. Peleliu, Battle of, Palau,
1944—Personal narratives. 5. World War, 1939-1945—Campaigns—Palau—Peleliu Island. 6. United States. Marine Corps—Biography. 7. Wolves—Wisconsin. 8.
Human-animal relationships. 9. Menominee Indian Reservation (Wis.)—Biography. 10. Wisconsin—Biography. I. State Historical Society of Wisconsin. II. Title.
  E99.M44K34 2014
  977.4004'973130092—dc23
  [B]
                            2014009149

To all members of the Menominee Nation:
May the Great Spirit smile on you often.

CONTENTS

FOREWORD

BY DR. S. VERNA FOWLER, FOUNDING PRESIDENT
COLLEGE OF MENOMINEE NATION

"Take only memories; leave nothing but footprints."
—*Chief Seattle*

In this personal history, Raymond Kaquatosh illustrates what life was like for a young American Indian boy growing up and maturing in the early 1900s on the Menominee Reservation. As he relates his early education in a boarding school, his teenage escapades, his barroom brawls, and his experiences as a US Marine, he also chronicles his experiences with the attitudes and beliefs of that era that perceived Indian people as stoics, fighters, and naturalists who possess a great sense of humor.

Despite those stereotypes, Ray developed into an independent individual, a living, thinking, feeling human being with a remarkable, even scholarly intellect and notable survival skills.

This memoir is must reading for all of us to aid our understanding of other cultures, particularly young American Indians growing up on reservations because it connects them with their elders. Ray Kaquatosh reminds us all that others have traveled the path before us, and therefore we are not victims of circumstance. We have choices, and others' footprints to follow, and because of that our lives are filled with hope and promise.

1

Birth of Little Hawk

It is July 25, 1924, and I am about to be born. No physician is present, but a Second Mother, or midwife, is summoned to participate. My parents are John and Margaret. John is half Chippewa and Menominee. Margaret is mostly Menominee.

Preceding my birth, my mother instructed my father and my Second Mother on any eventuality that might occur. They both have to participate in the rituals, offerings, and talks with the Great Spirit. My father must refrain from drinking alcoholic beverages. He cannot utter profanity and is to never disregard the Great Spirit in any manner. Sometimes a man with spiritual qualifications, a Shaman or Medicine Man, is called in to help with magical singing during a birth, but my mother refused this assistance. She knows the songs well enough on her own. She is a Medicine Woman, and the rules she sets are her own, different from those of other Menominee women.

With all this expert attention, who needs a doctor? Besides, doctors demand two dollars, which amounts to two days' pay, money my parents can't afford. Doctors never guarantee a safe delivery, anyway. They do not know the songs to sing to the Breath-Maker or how to ask the Great Spirit for assistance. The doctors tell you to cry out when pain is experienced, but this insults the spirits. Better to do it the Indian Way and be safe.

Like Mother Earth, my mother must not show signs of pain, fear, or distress while she gives birth. To express such things would displease the spirits. The child will be taken back to the Happy Hunting Ground, and bad things will also happen to the mother. My mother reminds herself that Mother Earth gives birth to various forms of life, such as flowers, grass, and trees, without showing signs of pain. A woman should feel grateful and be brave and strong during delivery, for it is the greatest moment of her life.

When the cord of life is severed, I give no sign of breathing. The Second Mother delivers a slap to my behind, and still my spirit does not respond. Mother sings a song to the spirits and asks for mercy. Then, speaking in Menominee, she prays, "Please let him breathe!"

Another slap is delivered, and I begin to bellow like a young buffalo. At this instant my mother says, "Thank you, Great Breath-Maker, for hearing my plea. I will be a good mother to this little one. Tomorrow I will make an offering to you, and the little one will be told of your generosity when he gets older."

———

All these facts were related to me in general discourse from my mother and my siblings as I grew older and more able to understand. As the kerosene lamps lit the room and the wood-burning stove radiated heat, these events were recalled and revealed to me.

My mother told me that I had a huge appetite when I arrived and had to be nursed immediately. I bellowed at the evil spirits for holding my breath and was quickly silenced by my first food from her breast. She told me I was distressed when I had to be moved from her left breast to her right breast. If I was first fed from her right side, the farthest from her heart, the spirits would be displeased. After giving me my initial nourishment, she noticed I had a happy face, and she smiled. She knew the Great Spirit smiled on both of us. At that precise moment, my Second Mother said, "I'll burn some cedar." She took up some cedar boughs and burned the tender green parts. This was done to ward off evil spirits.

After an Indian woman gives birth, it is customary that she stand up and try to walk. According to my mother, some women used to give birth in a squatting position. My mother had to get up lest the evil spirits arrive and force us to evacuate our dwelling. This is the Indian Way of being prepared for any eventuality, such as fire or smoke. After she became ambulatory, my mother craved a cup of wintergreen tea. As the tea was poured, she noticed a bird image in the vapors and knew I would be of the Aviary, or Bird, clan.

My Second Mother stayed for only one night. My mother, who weighed about one hundred pounds and was five feet tall, was too proud to have her stay any longer.

The home I was born in had no running water, electricity, or an indoor toilet. The only light we had at night was the kerosene lamp burning brightly. Our kitchen had a wood-burning stove, which was used for heating water at the time of my birth. In the winter the stove would be used to heat our home.

I spent the first few months of my life in a cradle that consisted of a flat board with a hoop on the top. It was padded and laced through eyelets on the sides to prevent me from sliding out while being transported. It had two adjustable shoulder straps. On the hoop were fringes of buckskin, beadwork, bone ornaments, and a padded hand grip. The hoop also served as a roll bar to prevent suffocation if the cradle was turned upside down. Indian mothers think of everything when it comes to the safety of their babies.

Each time the cradle was used by different members of the family, it had to be redecorated. My mother gave birth to four children before me and two children after me. This was convenient because there was always someone around to help us take care of one another.

Each of us kids had a song that was sung in Menominee. For fear it would lose its potency, the meaning of the words were never revealed to me. I was later told my song worked wonders and lulled me to sleep quicker than a sleeping pill and better than my brother's wine.

Because our home was heated by a wood-burning stove, during the first winter I slept with my parents. By morning, the fire would die and the temperature would drop below freezing. A little papoose like me could have frozen to death without a whimper.

My mother told me many stories of my infancy and often reminded me to be respectful toward the spirits and grateful for my well-being. She made offerings for me so that I would have a good future. What went into these offerings will never be revealed, because most people who do not understand the Indian Way scoff at it. I was taught to never criticize anyone's beliefs or religion.

When I was about two years old, I fell on the hot stove and burned my arm. The evil spirits must have pushed me when my mother wasn't looking. It was time to talk to the Creator and ask forgiveness. Offerings needed to be made for my safety.

During my third year, I needed new moccasins, mittens, and a cap, which were made of deerskin and beaded for ostentatious purposes. Many women envied my mother's beadwork, which she often sold.

In my fourth year I became adventurous. The Wolf River was just across the road from our home, and I was determined to get my feet wet. Thanks to my older brothers, I learned how to swim earlier than most. They threw me in the water and made no effort to help me out. After a few gulps of water, I began to successfully paddle my way out. Big brothers sure are helpful at times. I miss their benevolence like a toothache. I still think that they tried to kill me.

The forest around our home was dense with pine trees and small vegetation. One area, known as the Crow's Nest, was impossible to penetrate, so trails had been made there. One day I wandered along one of the trails and became so interested in the plants, chipmunks, birds, and butterflies that I soon became lost and tired, so I fell asleep. My family and many people from Neopit started looking for me. They found me curled up in a fetal position. My mother told me I didn't open my eyes on the way home. It was decided there would be no more trailblazing for me.

When I was five, my older siblings began preparing me for the start of first grade at the local school. There were no nurseries for the young or nursing homes for the old on the reservation. Each family provided for its members, and the nuclear family system prevailed until modernization. I was told, "Look out for the young and the old. Try to be helpful to the incapacitated." This way of life begins early and never seems to fade.

2

Reservation Boyhood

The year I started school, 1929, was also the start of a devastating economic disaster: the Great Depression. This catastrophic event lured men from far away to seek employment at the saw mill and logging camps near our home. It was not uncommon to see them walking along the roads begging for food and water. My mother never turned them down. Some were so grateful they kissed her hand, and some even cried.

My father had attended the Carlisle Indian Industrial School in Pennsylvania for a short time. With his advanced education, he became head of the time-keepers at the logging camps and was paid fifty dollars a month. The average camp laborer earned one dollar a day and worked seven days a week. Payday was every other week, and at that time my father would come home for a two-day rest. On these occasions he would have to trek five miles or more from the logging camps to the town of Neopit. Sometimes he would get a ride from men returning teams of horses to the barns in town.

The lumberjacks brought excitement to our area. They drove their cars to and from the towns nearby, and sometimes they drank too much and ended up driving into the river or against a tree. One day we heard a loud noise and saw a Model T on our front lawn. The driver wanted to know why our house was parked in the roadway. Then he tried to get out and fell on his ass, got up, and asked, "Who hit me?" He started dancing around like he was in a boxing match. My father got a bucket of water and threw it on his head. Then the man wanted to know when the rain stropped. My father answered, "Yesterday, and if you don't get that piece of junk off my lawn, there'll be a big storm right here." The man staggered back to his car and started to crank the engine. To my surprise, it started. He tried to get in the driver's seat but slipped and had to hold onto the steering wheel and pull himself up and into the seat. Then he backed over our lawn and across the highway, right into the river. He got out of the car and passed out on the riverbank. A few hours later he knocked on our door and said, "Someone stole my car." My father asked, "Do you have trouble parking?" The man said, "No." My father pointed at the river and replied, "Then why did you park it in the river?"

It took a team of horses to pull the car out.

The Depression kept my father busy figuring out the wages of the white men who came to work at the camps, and while most families suffered, ours prospered. This was because my father was a steady worker, and his bookkeeping was in demand. He never had to seek employment outside the reservation.

During this time my father had a new home built just about a mile east of Neopit along Highway 47. The home was furnished with a new cook stove, one with an oven on top and a water reservoir on one side. It even had a gauge on the door to indicate the temperature. On top it had six round removable lids. It was bought from Sears, Roebuck & Co. in Chicago.

Our front room was equipped with another stove, an upright

model made by Acme Sunburst. It was nickel-plated on top and the sides, with two doors on top and one smaller door on the bottom. The bottom door was used to remove ashes. This stove even had little windows to view the fire and had a footrest on the side.

We owned another luxury item, an ice chest consisting of an upright box with a large door in front. On top it had a lid that covered a reservoir for the ice. My parents' bed had brass ends, and each corner post had a big brass ball on top. This type of bed was considered in vogue because it was strikingly attractive, with graceful lines.

My father even bought a new Talking Machine, or phonograph. This contraption consisted of a box about four feet tall with a door in front and a lid on top to enclose the turntable. Along the side was a lever to stop or start the revolution of the turntable. There was also an arm that housed a needle. The arm pivoted, and when lowered onto the record it would produce music. The Talking Machine cost $14.95.

With new clothes, toys, and plenty of food, I couldn't ask for anything more. But one thing fascinated me more than any of my toys: that phonograph. One day when no one was looking, I managed to get the door to the record compartment open. I started to crawl up to the top and was pulled back out by my mother. She asked me, "What are you looking for?" I told her I was trying to find all those little people who made the music and sang. She laughed and tried to explain the functions of the Talking Machine. Also, she gave me a stern warning not to venture inside again, or my little behind would get a warming.

Our family was considered one of the more affluent in our

society. Yet my father never boasted. He went out of his way to help others and never tried to put them down. When people tried to put him down, it might cost them in the end. Here's what happened to him one day . . .

The 1929 Fords and Chevys were on display at one of the local dealerships in Shawano, and my father decided it was time to get rid of the old Model T. My father, eldest brother, and I drove to Shawano, entered a Ford garage, and approached a salesman. My father asked the salesman, "How much for the Ford?" The salesman replied, "Too much for you." My father reached into his pocket and produced four one-hundred-dollar bills, showed them to the salesman, and said, "On the way over here I couldn't decide what to buy, a Chevy or a Ford. You just made up my mind for me to buy a Chevy." He turned and walked out the door with the salesman begging him to reconsider.

I still remember that Chevy. It was a four-door with disc wheels and a spare attached under the back window. It was dark green and had a four-cylinder engine with a stick shift on the floor. Total cost was about $375. The Model T Ford we had earlier didn't have roll-up windows, and we got wet when it rained. But the Chevy had roll-up windows, and it even had a heater and a windshield wiper. What a car!

———

In the fall of 1929 I started my first year at the Neopit grade school. The school taught grades one through eight and had a gymnasium attached to it that served as a playground in the winter. Outside there were swings and a small, self-propelled merry-go-round.

The school was about a mile from our home, and we made the daily trek if weather permitted. Sometimes I had to be carried when I got tired.

As the leaves began to fade, so did our memories of the hot summer. This started the most spectacular season of all, when Mother Earth shows her colors, red, yellow, and gold. Sometimes we could hear flocks of geese honking as they winged southward. They seemed to be telling us winter was not far away. Some of us Indians believe that when geese start their migration early, winter will come sooner, and it will be long and hard. Their appearance also signaled to us to gather leaves and bring them to school to make decorations. We would trace the leaves on paper and color them.

After the first frost came Indian Summer. This warming trend gave us time to fill our larder and prepare for the long winter. After Indian Summer we anticipated the first snows. When they came, we knew we'd better have enough wood for the stove. Sometimes we could be snowed in for a month.

During October we made cutouts of black cats, witches on broomsticks, and pumpkins. They decorated the school windows, and we were allowed to bring some of them home. Soon we would draw pictures of pumpkins, turkeys, Pilgrims, and cornstalks in honor of the Harvest Feast. The white man calls this Thanksgiving, but my mother called it the ruination of the Indians. She said, "They should be giving thanks to the Indians for helping them through the first winter." She hated this time of year, but she always gave thanks to the Great Spirit for giving us a nice crop of vegetables, and she decorated our home with ears of Indian corn. Not all Menominee people believed as my family did or worshipped the Great Spirit in the manner we did, but I was taught to believe that everyone has the right to worship as they choose.

Not long after the Harvest Feast, Father Sky would cover the earth with a blanket of white. That winter of 1929 was the most difficult for me, because I still had to rely on my siblings to carry me when the snow was too deep. I missed a whole week of school, and finally I had to quit going to school entirely because no one wanted to carry me around.

My father came home for Christmas. He told us that he and some other men had encountered a timber wolf pack. The leader of the wolf pack had stopped and stared at my father and then ran away.

The Christmas of 1929 was significant to my mother because she would no longer speak to me in Menominee. "Learn to read and write the white man's language, and you'll never be sorry," she told me over and over again.

Things got easier for me in the spring of 1930, when my eldest brother started to drive the Chevy and it became his duty to get me to and from school. With his help, the first year of school seemed to pass quickly. My second year of school was almost identical, with the exception that I had more homework and was required to try to walk the mile and a half to school when the weather permitted it.

In the third year there were more books to carry and more studying required. It was tough trying to live like the white man. *Who needs this?* I thought. *Why not live like the Indian and hunt and fish for a living? It's much easier.*

That year my younger sister joined me at school. Her name

was Catherine, and now it was my responsibility to protect her. My little sister didn't have a dark complexion, and her hair was a lighter, reddish brown. But her eyes were almost the same as mine, dark brown, and her facial features resembled mine.

Catherine and I grew closer as we got older, and we always shared our toys. When our older brothers and sisters scolded her, she turned to me for comfort. We would run off somewhere and hide until the pain subsided. During the summer we explored the area around our home. We hunted frogs, turtles, minnows, birds, chipmunks, and butterflies along the Wolf River and the ponds near our home. Our mutual interests, loyalties, and affections bound us.

On the walk home from school, Catherine and I would throw stones in the river and watch the circles expand. We'd watch the trucks near the saw mill or the steam locomotive moving slowly toward the station. Sometimes we'd catch a glimpse of a squirrel jumping from branch to branch or watch a chipmunk scurry across the road. We heard the sounds of the woodpeckers pounding on a tree or the cry of a loon on the Wolf River. On the back trail, we heard the rustle of leaves, the whispers of pines, or just the sound of a soft summer breeze. Occasionally we heard the wolves howl, not uncommon during the early 1930s. All of this made the reservation an enchanting place.

Sometimes we took field trips along the Wolf River and paid a visit to the saw mill, where we watched the logs being cut into boards. Once we were taken to Spirit Rock on Highway 55 north of Keshena and were given a brief history of the rock. Many years ago, Spirit Rock began to crumble. When it gets to the point that it can no longer be seen, the Menominee people will also disappear. When standing near the rock, you possess spiritual powers and must concentrate, because the first thing you begin to imagine will become real.

Another main event in our year was the annual powwow at the Keshena Fairgrounds. We were told to observe the costumes worn by the dancers and listen to the songs being sung in Menominee.

These years were some of the happiest times of my life. But my mother always reminded me, "When things are going too smoothly, look out for the unexpected." Still, I never dreamed what was about to happen.

3

The Great Spirit Beckons

In the fall of 1932, my mother told me that my father was not feeling well and that he was coming home for a rest. He had a cough that would not subside. He gave up smoking for the time being, but this did not help. He was short of breath, felt weak, and was unable to walk even a short distance. After a thorough examination at the local hospital, the doctor informed my father that he had tuberculosis, and it was terminal. He was told to go back home and get plenty of rest. It was the beginning of the end for him.

We all helped take care of him, and that's what he appreciated most—that he was at home with his family to care for him. When he woke up from a nap, he would ask for a certain member of the family, and we'd be right there for a short talk. I think many times he was just checking on us to see if we were all right. This was his way of being protective.

After the holidays, the outlook was bleak. My mother started to prepare for the worst. She purchased enough provisions for the rest of the winter. As my father grew weaker, I was the one who had to provide wood for the small stove in the room where he suffered from coughing and chest pains. Sometimes while I was putting wood in the stove, he would say, "Raymond, I appreciate your efforts." Then I would gaze at his graying hair and hope he would get better soon. At times I would ask the Great Spirit to let him get up and walk around and be energetic.

We kept him warm all winter and tried to make him feel comfortable, but his cough got worse. Sometimes we had to help him get up, and other times my brothers and I had to carry him around and help him sit up. He must have known the Great Spirit was going to beckon, because one day he sat up by his own power and said, "I'm hungry." This startled my mother, and she quickly prepared a meal for him. He devoured the food and fell asleep.

It was his last meal.

The next day, he looked up at my mother and said, "I'm really tired." My mother started to cry. She stayed by his side all night. She never cried in his presence, and at the time I assumed that he never noticed it.

Early the next morning, my mother woke me and told me that my father was waiting to see me. As she pulled me along, she said, "Hurry!" With the kerosene lamp burning brightly by his bed, I could tell that he had more trouble breathing. He said, "I have to go now. Be a good boy." He reached out and shook my hand and smiled. His hand went limp, and he looked up, still smiling, as he took his last breath. I took one last look at his hair. It was the same color as a wolf. My mother pulled me aside and said, "Go back to bed." I asked, "Can't we get a scientist to bring him back to life?" My mother just looked at me and shook her head. She said, "He's with the Great Spirit now." Then she sat by my father until the kerosene lamp was out.

We shall meet again; it's only a matter of time.

My father was born on December 23, 1883, and died on April 16, 1933. This was marked on his cross at St. Anthony's

Cemetery, just about four blocks from our home. As an Indian, I was taught by my father never to cry for someone who has died. That is a sign of weakness. But I cried the day they buried him. During the burial service I had a hard time trying not to show weakness, and when I got home I ran off and cried for hours. I was afraid my family would find out and I would be disgraced, and I hoped my father would forgive me for being so weak. My mother sensed I had been crying and gave me a big hug and said, "It's all right to show sorrow, and no one will hold it against you." This made me feel better, and that's when I noticed my brothers showed signs of crying as well. I suddenly realized my little sister must have been crying, too. So I went to her and hugged her, trying to be cheerful. I glanced back at my mother, who made a half-smile at both of us.

From then on, I decided, I had to be more protective of my little sister. I had to show no fear of the future and be more helpful while my family made the necessary adjustments coping with the loss of my father. That is what he must have meant when he told me to be a good boy. I tried to be helpful with my mother and the rest of my family. Nevertheless, I still grieved, and I will always be grateful for having a wonderful father. My father never abused my mother, and I never saw him drunk. He was firm but fair and always listened to our point of view. He was tolerant with everyone.

My mother told me later she heard the wolves howling the night my father died. Maybe they were sad or saying good-bye. Maybe they were announcing something. Perhaps one among them was about to be born.

4

Poverty

The spring of 1933 was not too bad, as my mother had taken steps to provide canned food, flour, and other essentials to last us the rest of the winter. My eldest brother finished high school and started working at the logging camp. He helped support us for a short while, but then he became disillusioned. One payday he went on a drinking spree. This disgusted my mother and the rest of the family. Soon afterwards, he lost his job.

In the fall my mother couldn't afford new clothes for us, so we had to make do with the clothes we wore last year. Wearing old clothes was not too bad, but our lunches were a little skimpy. The better part of my lunch was a peanut butter and jelly sandwich made with homemade bread. My friends at school liked the thick slices of bread my mother made, and I had no problem trading it for a real meat sandwich!

One day the Great Spirit smiled on me. I was told to go to the hotel at lunch time. There I got a noon meal provided for me by my father's estate. These meals lasted until Christmas. Every time I finished eating there, I would save something for my little sister. Once a woman noticed me putting a cookie in a bag, and she asked, "Why are you putting a cookie in that bag?" When I told her it was because my little sister and I always shared our treats, she looked at me sadly and said, "Wait here, and I'll be back." When she returned, she handed me a bag full of cookies. From that day on she always had a bag of treats for me.

Without a car for transportation, I was forced to walk, and at times this was a dangerous task. Sometimes I would encounter a stray dog or some drunk driver. On the way home one day I noticed a car zigzagging toward me, so I ran behind a tree. To my surprise, the driver hit the tree next to me. The front end bounced up and came to rest at a forty-degree angle with the front end up like it was trying to crawl up the tree.

Living in poverty *and* trying to keep from getting run over by a Model T was getting to be too much for me.

5

Dillinger

It was the fall of 1933, and the leaves had fallen from the trees, leaving the branches naked. The leaves made a soft carpet of red and yellow on the ground, and it was fun to walk and kick through them. The cooler breeze made me scurry home from school. Once home, as I closed the front door, I noticed a black 1933 Ford approaching. Seeing this new car made me stop and wonder why it was pulling up to our home. My eldest brother had noticed it before I did. He called out to my other brother, "Get the shotgun! If they give us any trouble, shoot 'em!"

The driver got out and knocked on our door, saying, "I'd like to talk to you about getting a little sleep."

"Come in," said my brother at the door.

"Thanks," said the gentleman.

"Are you armed?" asked my brother.

"Why?"

"Because my brother has a shotgun aimed right at you. Look behind you!"

The man replied, "Hey, I mean no harm. All we need is some sleep. Here's a twenty . . ."

"You just bought yourself protection for the entire night," was my brother's reply.

Just then Willie Waukau from across the highway called out, "Tom, are you okay?"

"Yeah, Willie, it's just my uncle from out of town," answered my brother.

"You think he'll call the police?" the man at the door asked.

"No. If he pulls out, I'll call you," my brother said. "Now park your car in the back of the house, and get some sleep."

The man said, "Thanks. I'm dead tired. I really appreciate this."

"It's okay," my brother told him. "I hate cops."

"So do we," the man agreed.

The man who had stepped out of the Ford and knocked on our door was John Dillinger, and he displayed the most charisma of any man I've ever known. My mother even liked him, and she hated all white men!

Later that night my brother woke Dillinger and his men. They came into the house, all yawning and stretching. While they were rubbing their eyes, my brother handed them cups of coffee.

"That's the best coffee I've ever tasted," John said after taking a sip.

"It's made from spring water," my brother informed him. While the men were sleeping, my mother had cooked them a meal. She made Indian fried bread, American fried potatoes, and scrambled eggs, and she kept it all warm in the oven above the stove. After they devoured their meal, John showed the sort of etiquette found only in high society. Here's what he said to my mother: "That's the best-tasting bread I ever ate in my entire life."

My mother blushed at that and said, "Have another. And there's more in the oven."

"Ma'am, I can't thank you enough." He turned and pointed at me and asked my brother, "Who is this young man?"

"He's my kid brother, and his name is Ray."

John reached out and shook my hand and said, "My name is John."

"He's been listening for cars ever since you went to sleep," my eldest brother said.

"Do you like gum?" John asked me.

"Yes," I answered.

"Here's a pack of spearmint."

"Thanks!"

"And here's fifty cents for looking out for us."

"Thank you again."

"Now you have a friend for life," my brother told John.

"That's what I need, a friend. Thanks again," said John. He made me feel very important.

As he walked toward the door, he mussed up my hair, reached down to shake my hand, and said, "Thanks again."

I remember the taillights shining as John and his fellows slowly drove out of our driveway. They waved and honked the horn. As they went out of sight, my brother said, "I think they're headed for Little Bohemia."*

"I hope they make it," I said.

My mother added, "That's one damn nice white man."

I was told never to reveal this event to anyone, or I'd get a kick

---

* Little Bohemia, a lodge in Manitowish Waters, Wisconsin, was a Dillinger hangout and the site of an April 1934 shootout between the Dillinger gang and FBI agents. Dillinger was shot and killed by federal agents in Chicago in July 1934.

in the ass. No one would believe me if I told them I had met John Dillinger, even though it was a known fact around Neopit that he used the reservation as a sanctuary because the state police and nearby authorities had no jurisdiction on federal land. Only the FBI could intervene.

Dillinger might have been a fugitive, but he treated the Indians with great respect, and for that I will always respect him. I'll never forget the green wrapper on that Wrigley's spearmint gum package and the fifty-cent piece he gave me.

When John Dillinger was killed in Chicago, I felt like I lost a friend, one who had treated me with respect and appreciation. I hope the Great Spirit was as kind to him as he was to the Indians.

6

Keshena Boys' School

After Christmas of 1933 my mother took me aside and tried to explain that she could no longer afford to keep me at home. I was to be sent to the government school[*] in Keshena, eleven miles from our home.

When my little sister heard this, she started to cry, and I couldn't do anything to ease her pain. She cried herself to sleep that night, but I was too angry to let this make me any more upset. My brothers could have been sent there instead of me, but they refused to go. It seemed like I was the sacrificial lamb, and this was the beginning of my feelings of hatred toward them. When I noticed my mother crying, I put my arm around her and said, "Don't cry. I'll be all right." She turned, and I could see her sadness. "There's no food, and your brothers are out of work. There's nowhere to turn for money," she told me. "At least in the boys' school you'll have a clean bed and food. You'll also have new clothes." All this meant nothing to me. I was bitter and couldn't wait for the policeman to come pick me up and take me away.

When the policeman arrived, he asked, "Who will be going to the Keshena boys' school?" My mother pointed me out. Too

---

[*] The Menominee Boarding School at Keshena merged with the Catholic-run St. Joseph's Indian Industrial School in 1933.

angry over this turn of events, I just started walking toward the car without saying good-bye. Then I heard my little sister cry out for me. I knew I had to go back and console her. I asked the policeman, "Please let me go say good-bye to my sister." He nodded and said, "Of course, take your time. I'm in no hurry." I thanked him.

I walked back to Catherine's room and tried to convince her that I would be all right. "Who will take care of me?" she asked.

"We'll all help," my mother said, "and Ray will be back on the weekends." My sister didn't seem convinced. I just gave her a hug and turned to walk out the door.

On the way to Keshena, the policemen asked me, "How come you didn't cry?"

"I'm Indian, and we don't show weakness. Only women cry."

"I'm Indian, too, and I cry sometimes."

"You must be part white man."

"Don't get funny now."

"I'm not trying to be funny. My parents taught me to be strong and never cry like the white man."

The policeman began to tell me about his boyhood and how he had to go to the same school in Keshena and had cried at times because he was never visited by his parents. They had both died when he was my age. It was comforting to hear him talk about how rough his childhood was. He said, "This school is not that bad."

The bumpy, gravel-road ride from Neopit to Keshena seemed to take hours, and I was glad when the policeman pointed toward some brick buildings and said, "There's your new home." He parked in front of a building with wide steps leading to a big door. At the top of the steps was a huge white man. He must have weighed about three hundred pounds. He introduced himself.

"Hi, I'm Mr. Shea, and I'll be one of your teachers and your dorm master."

As Mr. Shea led me toward the laundry room, I could feel the floor shake with his every step. He reached for the shelves and started to hand me clothes, towels, and soap. He pointed at the shower room and said, "Go take a shower, and see me when you get all cleaned up."

When I entered the shower room, I noticed a long row of toilet seats. Hey, these white men had indoor plumbing! They sure had it easy. They even had running water indicated by knobs: one for hot, the other cold. The hot knob seemed to be the one to turn, and when I did, the warm water started to rain on my face. The water got hotter and hotter until I could no longer stand it. This was the first shower I ever had. I waited for the water to cool down, but it never did.

Now that I knew how to take a shower, I had to try out the toilet. So I dropped my pants and was sitting with hands cupped around my chin when some smartass hit the flush button, and I flew off the seat like I'd been kicked by a mule.

I headed to Mr. Shea's room. When I entered, he asked, "How was your shower?" I told him that the water got too hot. He smiled and told me how to make it cooler or warmer. After showing me to my bed and locker, Mr. Shea said, "If you feel lonesome and start crying, my door is always open." I told him, "Indian boys in our family don't cry." He smiled and said, "Well, if you do, I won't tell anyone." Then he put his hand on my shoulder and told me about some of the other boys who had lost their parents to the Happy Hunting Ground.

When the Great Ball of Fire went to hide and darkness covered the earth once again, here's what happened to me. At first the dormitory was filled with laughter from boys having pillow fights and chasing each other around, but when the lights were turned off, I could hear sobbing. I was determined not to show weakness like the white man, but I must confess that the evil spirits must have put some irritant in my eyes, causing them to emit tiny drops. These drops would have disgraced me if my father could have seen them. I told myself, *I must be brave and show courage and be able to overcome these trivial circumstances. After all, am I not an Indian?*

The beds at the school were so high that I had to jump up to get on top of mine. My first attempts proved embarrassing. I took a running jump, but the momentum forced me to fall over the other side, and I landed right on my rear. I laughed so hard, I cried. Mr. Shea heard the noise and turned on the lights. He came over to my bed and asked why I was laughing. I told him I fell out of bed. "You fell out of bed?" Everyone in the dorm started laughing. I couldn't tell anymore who was crying or laughing. Mr. Shea's belly started to shake, and that made me laugh even harder.

When the lights were turned off again, I gazed out the window and looked up at Father Sky. I saw the moon emerging from behind a cloud, and that seemed to tell me that I was not alone. This lonely night would soon pass, and tomorrow would be another day.

In the morning, we scurried to make our beds and rushed to the washroom with towels on our shoulders. The hot and cold running water woke us up even more. Yes, these white men sure had it easy. After we finished washing our hands and faces, we had to go outside and wait in the cold for Mr. Shea's inspection. After he had a good look at us, he'd say, "Follow me," and we'd head to the dining hall. The dining hall was equipped with tables that were put together to form a long row with neatly placed plates and utensils. In the middle of the tables was a grand display of steaming food. While we all stood by the tables, I was tempted to take a small morsel. But the nuns were watching, and if we were caught taking food before prayers, we would be reprimanded. The prayer we said before meals was to thank God for our food. I just thanked the Great Spirit, never realizing that they were one and the same. After the prayer, we were told to sit and eat. We had fresh milk, oatmeal, biscuits, and even black coffee. These white men sure knew how to eat. No wonder they got so fat!

After breakfast, we went to the classrooms and began the drudgery of trying to understand the ways of the civilized world. What a waste of time! But some of the books we read were interesting and had a lot of pictures. Soon I grew interested and became involved in class projects that required me to read.

When Friday came, the other boys were being picked up by their families. Soon the dormitory was empty. What a lonely place! As I stood by the window peering at the last students leaving, I felt a hand on my shoulder and looked up to see Mr. Shea's sad eyes. "Sometimes I get lonesome on weekends, too," he said. Maybe I wasn't all that alone after all. He showed me to his office, took some books off the shelf, and handed them to me. He pointed to a radio and turned a knob, then turned another knob, and soon we would hear music coming from a far-off place called Milwaukee—radio station WTMJ. What more could I hope for?

The next morning, on the way to the dining room, Mr. Shea told me he had a surprise for me. After we entered the hall, I noticed there were no plates set at the other tables, but on the staff's table there were candles burning and a place set for me on the end. After we said our prayers, the nuns served us eggs and bacon. This would occur only when no one else was staying at the school over the weekend. It made me feel like I was someone special, and I knew I'd better show my gratitude. So after breakfast, I helped take the dishes back to the pantry. After I finished, one of the nuns gave me cookies. I thought, *The Great Spirit sure is looking out for me. When I get outside, I'd better look up and thank him.*

On the way back to the dormitory, I hopped and kicked and hummed a song of appreciation. What a life! This must be part of the Happy Hunting Ground. I had cookies in my pocket, a radio to listen to at night, books to read at any time, and I could leave the lights on at night. This was one of the most pleasant weekends I'd had in months! But it might be the calm before the storm, so I knew I'd better watch it.

After I returned to the dormitory, Mr. Shea approached me and asked, "Do you like cows?" I told him that I'd never had the opportunity to get close to one. He pointed toward the barn on the hill and said, "Go up there and tell Mr. Ladd to show you around."

As I sauntered to the barn, I thought about my family and wondered if they had enough to eat. Then I realized I couldn't share any of my cookies with my little sister. My thoughts of my family came to an abrupt end when I opened the large door to the barn and came face to face with the largest animal I had ever seen: a bull that must have weighed two thousand pounds! He lowered his head, snorted, and glared at me. I slowly backed toward the door and, as soon as I got outside, slammed it shut and ran away. As I was running around the building, I noticed a small door, opened it, and hollered for Mr. Ladd, but he didn't respond. So I headed back to the dorm, thinking, *This is what my mother warned me about. Indian mothers must know everything. Better thank the Great Spirit for saving me!*

Halfway back to the dorm, I met some men rushing toward the barn. One of them shouted, "Stay away from the barn! A bull is loose!"

"I know. He's with the cows," I replied.

One of the men paused to say, "You could've been killed!"

"That's why I'm running back to the dorm!" I said.

When I got back, I told Mr. Shea that I still hadn't gotten to see any cows, and I couldn't find Mr. Ladd because a bull was loose. "How do you know?" Mr. Shea asked.

"I opened the big door to the barn, and the bull was just standing there."

Mr. Shea gasped, "My God, you could've been killed."

I said, "That's why I'm not going back."

At dinnertime I met Mr. Ladd, and he told Mr. Shea and me that the bull had gotten loose but was now back in his pen. Then Mr. Shea asked him if he would show me around.

After dinner I strolled back to the barn and located the door to the milk house. I entered and saw Mr. Ladd pouring milk into a silver can. He smiled and said, "We have some new calves in the barn." He pointed into the direction of the bullpen.

"Are they mean?" I asked.

"Oh, gentle as a lamb," he replied

A calf walked toward me, and I began to pet it. Then Mr. Ladd hollered, "Look out!" I felt a hard bump to my behind and went flying toward the door, but without wings. "I forgot to warn you about that one," Mr. Ladd said. "Thanks," I replied.

When I got back to the dorm, I told Mr. Shea what I thought about mean cows. He told me that some get mean when a person gets too close to their young. "Now you tell me," I grumbled. My mother hadn't told me that trouble could come in bunches. Maybe Indian mothers don't know everything.

Later, as I was leafing through a book, Mr. Shea asked me, "Do you like cracklins?" I responded that I had never heard of them. He told me to go to the rear of the dining room and ask one of the nuns to give me some.

With hands in my pockets, I walked over to the dining room and asked the first nun I saw for some cracklins. She asked, "Do you like cracklins?" I shrugged and said, "Ain't never had any before." The nun corrected me, "Don't say *ain't*. Always say: *I haven't*." I nodded and said, "Well, I *haven't*." She smiled and said, "That's better. Now here's a bag of cracklins."

When I got back to the dorm, I handed the bag to Mr. Shea, and he said, "That's not for me, it's yours." So I opened the bag. What I took out resembled a potato chip, only it was much thicker. After eating a few, I knew why they called them cracklins—because they made a crackling sound in my mouth. When Mr. Shea told me that they were made of pork skins, I almost barfed. At least they tasted good.

The first week at the school taught me a few things: how to take a shower and make the water hot or cold, how to get on the bed without falling off, how I should say a prayer before I eat, how to look out for smartasses when sitting on the toilet, how to get music to play on the radio, and how I should stay away from the bullpen. The school amazed me. There was no wood stove to keep us warm and no kerosene lamps for light. You just pushed a button and the heat came on and pushed another and the lights came on. These white men sure had it easy.

7

Lonely Valentine

With January came the snows. The next two weekends I had plenty of company at the school, because no one wanted to get stranded on their way home. This ruined my chances to listen to the radio and keep the lights on at night.

Now, turning a bunch of Indian boys loose without supervision is inviting disaster to any classroom. We were told not to get into any trouble, but this was like telling wolves not to howl. Someone spilled ink on the teacher's desk, someone else drew pictures on the blackboard, and others tipped over the wastebasket and started to throw erasers at each other. It was time for me to get out of there. I retreated to the solitude of the dorm. Some of the boys were permitted to go up to the barn. I felt sorry for that mean cow and her calf. The boys even forced the bull to retreat to the outside area when they started to throw stones at him and scored a few hits.

By February the teachers were talking about a groundhog that could predict the weather. If it emerged from its den on February the second and saw its shadow, this meant we'd have six more weeks of winter. The white men sure have some funny beliefs.

February also brought Valentine's Day, and we had to start making paper hearts and draw a little naked man with a bow and arrow. His name was Cupid. That little guy must have been hanging around with some Indians and fraternized with a Medicine Man, because if he shot you with an arrow, you'd get love sickness.

That weekend, when the dorm was empty again, I slowly walked back to my locker and took out all my Valentines. As I started to tear them up and throw them into the wastebasket, I heard a familiar voice behind me say, "Save some for me." I thought, *How can a three-hundred-pound white man sneak up on a quiet little Indian boy who has good hearing, good eyesight, and the ability to outsmart a two-thousand-pound bull?* These white men amazed me at times. As I tore up another card, Mr. Shea said, "Those would be nice for my girls." He told me that he had two daughters and hadn't had a chance to buy them any Valentine's cards. I knew he was trying to cheer me up, so I gave him the rest of my cards and said, "Maybe you can get rid of the rest for me."

He walked slowly toward his room, and I followed him. I asked when he would get to see his girls again. He answered, "Not until Easter vacation time." He looked sad, and for the first time I felt sorry for him. Even if he was a white man, he showed compassion for all the boys. Now it was my turn to show my consideration for him and forget about the trivial things around this school. As we wrapped the cards and placed them in a small box, he said, "On holidays I get lonesome, too." He told me that sometimes he wanted to quit and go home, but he needed the money. He told me that sometimes he would cry himself asleep. "I'll never tell anyone," I told him. He began to laugh so hard his belly started shaking, and I knew he was happy.

The next day Mr. Shea said, "Good news! We're going to the big city of Shawano to have supper in a real restaurant and do some window shopping."

"What's window shopping?" I was hoping we weren't going to buy a lot of windows.

"It means you look in the store windows and not buy anything." I smiled. "That I can afford. Let's go."

We arrived in Shawano and parked in front of a restaurant called Uneeda Lunch. Mr. Shea ordered a hamburger and Coke for me. When the waitress served us a bunch of hamburgers on a tray, I thought we were going to have company. She took one off the tray for me and gave the rest to Mr. Shea—all *four* of them! When I began to eat one of the hamburgers, I found that the meat was so thick inside the bun that it was difficult to take a bite out of it. "Put some ketchup on it!" Mr. Shea said. So I took off the lid from the bottle and poured this red stuff on top of the meat, not knowing that the cook must have already put some on the bottom. When I picked it up, the meat shot out the other end of the bun and bounced onto my plate. Mr. Shea laughed, "That must have been a mean cow." After eating about half my sandwich, I looked at Mr. Shea's plate and saw there was only one burger left. I thought he must have dropped some on the floor. I looked around but couldn't find any.

The hamburgers and soda cost five cents each, so Mr. Shea gave the waitress seventy-five cents and told her to keep the change. I thought he must be the richest man in the world to give her forty cents for a tip.

We walked down Main Street and saw a lot of stores with clothing for men, and then we crossed the street to look at more items in the windows. We were getting near the Crescent Theatre when Mr. Shea asked, "Do you want to go see a movie?" I almost answered, "I ain't never seen one," but I remembered what the nun said about using the word *ain't,* so I corrected myself and said, "I haven't gone to a movie in my whole life."

He smiled and replied, "Well, you're about to."

In my young life I had realized early on that the white man was peculiar at times, but after watching this movie Mr. Shea took me to, I was convinced that they were all crazy. The title of the movie was *Monkey Business,* and it starred the four Marx Brothers.

One of the brothers wore big black glasses, one played the harp, one played the piano, and the other tried to sing. Their names were Groucho, Harpo, Chico, and Zippo. They made beautiful music but displayed irreverent mania and pure foolishness. Their antics made Mr. Shea's belly shake, and watching him laugh made me laugh even more.

Valentine's Day had not been so lonesome after all.

8

House of God

The weeks before Easter made me feel a little confused. We had to study something called catechism, and it was getting so profound that it required us to take a few excursions to the church. The nuns could understand what the priests said in Latin, but they could never explain why they sang and spoke it during the church services. They told us it was a dead language, and this confused us even more, but we had to accept it. On the walls were pictures of a man carrying a cross. No one seemed to be helping him with this burden. The nuns said he was carrying this for our sins and that he died for our sins as well. I thought there must have been some awfully bad white men.

We were never taken up to the balcony or shown where the bell was housed, because everyone was afraid we'd climb up there and fall out. At the front of the church was an altar with a rail that stretched from one side to the other. The nuns referred to it as the Communion rail. Each Sunday, people would kneel there and receive the Holy Eucharist. Everything was going smoothly until I mentioned that the Great Spirit would never tolerate these deplorable conditions. At this, a little nun's face turned red. "There is no such thing as the Great Spirit!" she screamed. "You are never to mention that name again."

Sunday morning after breakfast I was taken to the church near the school. A lot of people were hurrying to get to their seats. Some nuns were walking toward the back of the church where they would enter, walk by the altar, kneel, and make the sign of the cross over their chests. Then they would follow one another to occupy the first pews. When the bell began to toll and everyone stood up as the priest entered, Mr. Shea pulled me to my feet. Everyone kept standing up, kneeling, or sitting only to stand back up again. I was getting confused. I stood up when I was supposed to sit and knelt when I was supposed to stand. Once I knelt and was quickly pulled back to my seat by Mr. Shea. *Sure wish these white men would make up their minds,* I thought.

Then I heard voices from heaven. The choir began to sing. I thought they were angels because I couldn't see them standing up above me in the balcony. As the choir sang, here came the good part: someone passed a basket full of money in front of me! I reached to take some, only to have my arm pulled back by Mr. Shea, who said, "You're supposed to put some money *in,* not take it *out.*" When the basket was put back near the altar, the priest said that the money was for the poor and needy. I tugged on Mr. Shea's arm and said, "I'm poor and needy. So when will I get some of that money?" His stomach began to shake as he laughed, and when he couldn't stop laughing he had to excuse himself from church. These white men sure were peculiar at times.

It was Palm Sunday, and the upcoming week was called Holy Week. On this Sunday, we took some palm leaves home. They resembled yellow strips of paper that had been dried. The next Sunday would be Easter, which was the day the man on the cross, Jesus Christ, supposedly had come back to life. It was called the

Resurrection. I knew all of this because the nuns had been telling us about it all week.

Before spring vacation, we also had to prepare for the Easter Bunny. The nuns colored chicken eggs and filled small baskets with pieces of candy called jelly beans. The black jelly beans reminded me of rabbit droppings, so I hardly ate any black ones. The little nun who had turned red when I mentioned the Great Spirit told us about the big Easter egg hunt coming soon. I wanted to tell her that rabbits don't lay eggs, but I was afraid she'd turn red again. So I pretended to believe in the Easter Bunny.

Now, get this: one day we had to go out and look for Easter eggs. To my surprise, some kids found a few, and I thought, *Hey, I better get going* . . . I started to look near the trees and found one. Maybe these white men weren't so dumb after all. I couldn't wait to get home and tell my mother that all these years we had missed out on the Easter Bunny.

One day later that week, just before class, a boy named Jim gave me a cigarette and told me to smoke it, or I'd be called a sissy. I puffed it for a while, and then I felt really sick. When we returned to class, I felt even worse, and I turned to Jim and said, "That cigarette is making me sick." The little nun yelled at me to be quiet, but I got up, stuck my tongue out, and ran for the restroom. When I got back to the class, the teacher hit me on the head with a book. Talking in class and running out of class were big no-nos. Later I punched Jim in the nose.

On Good Friday all the other boys were picked up. Mr. Shea said, "We'll be alone again tonight, so you can listen to the radio and leave the lights on as long as you want."

I began to wonder why my mother wouldn't come to pick me up. The thought of running away from the school sounded good to me, but who would give me a ride to Neopit? If I got caught I'd be sent to school in Green Bay.

I decided to wait for summer vacation.

9

The Hospital

Just as I decided not to go over the north wall, I asked Mr. Shea if he was going home for the coming week. With a smile, he said, "Yes." When I looked at the ground, he put his hand on my shoulder and told me, "I've got good news for you."

"I'm being kicked out of school?"

"No, you're not that lucky. You'll be staying at the hospital with your own room for the whole Easter week."

"But I'm not sick."

"You don't have to be." He gave me a dollar and said it was "spending money" for the gift shop.

The next morning he took me to the hospital in Keshena and told me to be polite to the nuns because they were under a lot of stress trying to take care of all the sick people there. *Maybe they are trying to understand why the Indians don't like white men,* I thought to myself. We entered the front door, and a giant nun in a white habit approached us. She informed us that she was the Mother Superior. This meant that she was the top ranking pill-pusher in this whole outfit. As I followed them toward my room, I was wishing they wouldn't walk side by side, because the floor really began to shake underneath their combined weight, and I feared the building might come down on us.

The Mother Superior said I could walk all over the hospital, but the operating room was off limits. Damn it! Now I couldn't watch the sawbones in action. Mr. Shea started walking toward the door and gave me his final instructions on how to behave. He asked, "You still got that dollar I gave you?"

"Right here, next to my jackknife."

"Jackknife!" Mr. Shea exclaimed. "Better give me that, or they might kick you out of here."

Now the fun began. I had the entire hospital to explore and an entire week to do it. I started with the elevator. Let's see now . . . The little buttons read 1, 2, and Basement. So I pushed 2, then went back to 1. When the door opened on 1, a man in a white uniform was standing there with the Mother Superior. He had what appeared to be a little headlight on his head and a black cord around his neck with a small microphone on the end of it. The Mother Superior told me that he was the house doctor. I didn't know that houses had doctors.

"My office is over here," he said as he pointed toward his office and examining room. After I entered the room, he told me, "Sit on that table and take your shirt off."

He took the black cord from around his neck and put the ends in his ears, placed the little microphone on my chest, and demanded, "Cough." I coughed. The doctor scolded, "Not in my face! Now stick out your tongue."

"I can't do that."

"Why not?"

"It's not polite."

"Did you have a B.M. today?"

"What's a B.M.?"

"Your bowels . . . did they move?"

"Only when I jumped or ran." (I thought he meant my balls!)

"Take a deep breath and hold it."

After holding my breath for a minute or two, I started to get dizzy and almost fell to the side of the table. I coughed and gasped for air.

"Well, you didn't have to hold your breath for that long. Open your mouth and say ahh!"

I opened my mouth and went, "ahh, ahh, ahh, ahh, ahh."

"You can stop that now."

"Thanks," I laughed, "I was running out of ahhs."

He then pulled out a little hammer that looked like a tiny tomahawk and told me to relax. He bent over closer to me and hit me on the knee. I involuntarily kicked his chest and broke his pocket thermometer.

"Sorry," I said, "but you hit me first."

"That's okay, you have good reflexes."

"Thanks."

"You're a bright and fine young man."

"Tell that to the nuns at school, please."

"You can go back to your room now."

"Thank you. I only have a dollar to pay you."

"No charge."

Now I could explore the second floor and look for the gift shop. As I walked toward the elevator, I could hear chimes and cymbal-like bells. Then I heard the Mother Superior say, "Dinnertime!" She motioned for me to head toward the basement. As we approached a big room, I noticed a sign above the door that spelled out C-A-F-E-T-E-R-I-A. I hoped it didn't have anything to do with the cows in the barn.

Inside the room were tables covered with white cloths and chairs with soft pads to sit on, but there were no plates on the tables. How were we going to eat? Then I noticed a long line of people who were picking up dishes, forks, spoons, and knives. Okay, that's for me! I jumped in line, but I couldn't reach the utensils. A lady was behind me in a white dress and cap. She wore a mask, and I wondered if she had bad breath.

She lowered her mask and said, "Let me help you." She smiled, asking me what I would like.

"Some food!" I answered.

"Beef? Pork? Wieners?"

"Just pork. I can't eat all that."

"Potatoes and gravy? Potato salad?"

"Potatoes and gravy."

"Peas? Corn? Beets?"

"Peas."

"Jell-O? Sherbet? Ice cream?"

"What's sherbet?"

"It's like ice cream."

"I'll take some."

She helped me load my plate and then asked, "Would you like to sit with me?"

"Are you going to examine me?"

"No."

"Then I'll sit with you."

"What are you doing here?" she asked.

I told her I became a guest there because no one was left at school to take care of me. She looked at me as if she was about to cry. She told me she worked at the hospital and invited me to stop by and say hello.

"Where do you work?"

"The operating room."

"Sorry. It's off limits," I told her.

When she took off her cap, I could see that her hair was not unlike the color of the yellow Easter egg I had found.

Soon I was back to exploring this house of pain and suffering and at the same time trying to stay clear of the Mother Superior. Back to the elevator and up to the sunroom. I thought, *Hey, this is living! Maybe if I'm extra good I can stay a little longer.* As I walked past a half-open door, I could see someone standing with her back to me. I stopped to look. She didn't have any bottoms on, and the whole back of the garment was wide open. Times were bad, but the least they could do for sick people was give them a full set of pajamas! When she bent over, I got mooned for the first time in my life. As she settled into bed and pulled the covers up to her chest, she noticed me and screamed. I got the hell out of there, fast. *This must be the loony bin,* I thought. No more looking into rooms.

I came to the sunroom at last. Remembering I could leave the lights on late, I searched for some books with pictures in them to take back to my room. As I looked around, I saw a woman sitting at one of the tables. She turned and looked at me with sad eyes and asked me why I was there.

"I better not tell you," I answered.

"It's that bad, eh?"

"No, but you're a woman, and you might start crying."

"I knew it."

"It's not that bad."

"You're so brave."

"I'll make it."

"Here's a little something for you." The woman handed me a dollar bill and rushed out of the room crying. I knew white men were peculiar, but I began to believe that the women were even worse.

What a place! There were *Popular Mechanics* magazines with lots of pictures of cars. And I had two dollars in my pocket, more money than I'd had in my whole life. Who needs to go home when you've got all of this? Maybe the Great Spirit hadn't forgotten me after all! *Tonight I will go talk to him and ask forgiveness for all of my sins and promise not to punch anyone else's nose.*

But having money in your pocket and no place to spend it is as bad as not having any. I thought, *Maybe I can ask the Good Mother to let me go to the store in Keshena.* She beat me to the punch, though. When I saw her a little later, she told me to go to the gift shop and tell the woman there to give me an Easter basket.

I was hopping, skipping, and jumping when I got out of the elevator, and I tried to hit the low-hanging sign by the gift shop. I walked up to the counter, and the lady there handed me a basket. I didn't even have to ask for it. When I got back upstairs, I gave the basket to the Mother Superior, and she said, "Oh, no, that's not for me. It's yours. Happy Easter, Raymond!" With my jaw dropped and my eyeballs about to pop out of my head, I said, "For me? Gee, you're just like my mother. I wish I could stay here forever!" At that, the evil spirits must have put some irritant in the

Mother Superior's eyes, because they began to get a little wet and she reached into one of her sleeves and pulled out a handkerchief to blow her nose.

After I closed the door to my room, I took out some of the candy from the basket and found chocolate bunnies, chocolate eggs, and jelly beans. I even ate some of the black ones.

The next day I told the Mother Superior that I wanted to go to church and thank the good Lord for giving me all these presents, but I had only coveralls and didn't think they would allow me in on Easter Sunday. I also couldn't go all by myself.

"Don't worry, I've sent out for some nice clothes for you, and you can go with me."

"But I don't know when to stand, sit, or kneel."

"You'll sit with me, and I'll help you," she told me. These nuns were really smart, and the Mother Superior must have been the smartest of them all. She had an answer for every problem I had. *Maybe she can help me with my family,* I thought, *but I'm sure she has too many problems here with the sick. Especially that one with no back on her pajamas!*

10

Easter Sunday

Hours before church, the nuns started getting me dressed in my new attire. This included tying and untying my bowtie to their expectations. Then they combed my hair and parted it on the right side, then the left side, until finally I told them to just part it in the middle. The final inspection was by Mother Superior just before she went down to the cafeteria. She said I looked angelic, whatever that meant, and she sent me on my way to an early morning breakfast.

The church was located on the other side of Highway 47, and we had to walk from the hospital to the church, which was about four city blocks away. The Mother Superior took me by the hand and started to walk toward the church. I looked behind and saw about a dozen nuns following us in single file, Indian style, like a line of white mother ducks crossing the street. As we approached the highway, I noticed a few cars headed toward us. I hoped the Good Mother would stop and permit them to pass, but she had paid no attention to them and proceeded to cross right in front of them. To my surprise, the cars started slowing down, and some came to a complete stop.

We entered the church and walked straight toward the altar. We stopped at the pews next to the altar, crossed our chests, then entered the pews, knelt for a minute, thanked the Lord, and sat down. *I'm not doing too badly, no mistakes so far,* I thought. I took a peek at the nuns on my left. They wore black habits, and the Mother Superior wore white. *Hmmm, we must be the good guys,* I thought. Then the priest entered, and we all stood up. I noticed the priest was also wearing white, so he must be on our side. I wondered what the nuns in black would say when they found out I'd been fraternizing with the nuns in white.

When it came time to sit again, the Mother Superior sat and pulled me down with her, and so I sat as the rest of the congregation started to sit. Every time the Good Mother stood or knelt, everyone else followed. She sure had a lot of power, and I guess they didn't want to make her angry. They didn't even pass the collection basket in our pew.

The angels started to sing, and I turned to see if I could get a glimpse of them, but the Good Mother turned my head back, and I knew I had goofed again. Then the priest wrapped his hands in his white garment and took out a gold object and held it high. Everyone bowed their heads, except for me. I took a good look at that pretty object the priest held and wanted to keep looking up at it, but the Good Mother pushed my head back down. The priest told us to be good to our brothers and sisters. I began to wonder if my sister was all right, so I prayed to my Creator to be kind to her.

When the Mass was over, everyone started to leave, but we had to remain standing. I thought we must have done something wrong. Soon the Good Mother pulled at my arm, and we started to leave. Once we got outside and started down the steps, I told the Good Mother I was sorry that I goofed in church. But to my surprise she said, "You did just fine."

As we approached the highway again, I didn't even bother to look left or right for cars. We walked straight ahead, and all the cars slowed and came to a halt again. The Great Spirit must have had his arm around us all that time, because I could hear tires squealing.

Once we arrived back at the hospital, I asked if I could take off my bowtie. The Good Mother asked why. I told her that it was choking me. "Why didn't you say something earlier?" she asked. I told her I was afraid that if I didn't wear it, I would not be able to go to church. She bent down and with her big hands began to loosen my tie. Then she said, "I'm proud of you, Raymond." Later she told me if I ever needed help, all I had to do was call her.

When we got near the elevator, I could smell the ham cooking and I began wishing dinner was ready. Just to pass the time, I walked by the gift shop, but it was closed. They must have run out of Easter baskets, but who needs them, anyway? I had a few chocolate eggs left, and besides, I wanted to save some money for school next week.

A little later I heard the chimes, and I knew the long wait was over. I headed toward the basement and stood in line with a lot of people who were all wearing masks over their mouths. I hoped that they wouldn't get too close to me. But then a horrible thought came to me: without their help, who would help me get food? I lucked out—the nurse standing in line behind me didn't have a mask on. Now all I had to do was ask her to help me get a tray and some food.

Once inside the dining room, I noticed that no one was standing in line by the big window. Now what? But then I saw, to my surprise, that all the tables had food and plates on them. Everyone stood and said prayers. Next they all started to fill their plates. I couldn't reach the food, so I just sat and watched.

"Aren't you going to eat?" asked the nurse.

"I'd like to, but I can't reach the food."

"I'm sorry. Let me help you."

She started to heap my plate full of potatoes and gravy and ham. I had to stop her from putting too much on my plate. "Not too much—I can't eat all that, and it's a sin to waste good food."

She smiled and handed me the plate of food. As I was about to eat, a horrible thought came to mind. I worried my family was not having as good a dinner as this. I hoped they would have a good meal. I had faith that the Great Spirit would not let me down. So I ate. After I finished, I settled myself in my room and was about to begin reading a magazine when I heard a knock on my door. When I opened it, I saw a small nun standing there with her hands tucked into her sleeves. She asked if she could come in, and I obliged. She introduced herself and asked me if I could do her a great favor.

"Well," I told her, "if it's okay with the Mother Superior, it's okay with me. What can I do?"

"Follow me, and I'll tell you."

On the way to the second floor, she informed me about a sad boy who was lonesome for his mother, and she asked if I would try to cheer him up. "I'll try," I promised.

When we entered the boy's room, I noticed his eyes were all red. He tried to smile, but he must have been in pain because he couldn't smile very well. The little nun said, "Bobby, this is Ray. He's come to visit you for a little while."

The sad boy and I greeted each other.

"Why are you here?" Bobby asked.

"To keep you company," I answered.

"No, I mean, why are you in the hospital?"

"I was in the boys' school, and everyone left, so they had to bring me here until school opens again tomorrow."

"Don't you have a home?"

"Yes, but my father died and my mother can't afford to keep me at home."

"Gee, that's tough."

"Oh, it's not so bad. Someday I'll go back home."

"When did you see your mother last?" he asked.

"After Christmas."

"You mean you haven't seen her since?"

"I haven't seen any of my family since I got here," I told him.

"Don't you get lonely?"

"Sure. But I never cry."

"Why?"

"Because only white men and girls cry. I am an Indian."

Bobby begged to differ. "But I'm Indian, and I cry."

"Better not," I told him, "or the Great Spirit won't like you."

After I had talked with Bobby for a while, he told me that his mother had forgotten about him, and it really hurt, so that's why he was crying.

"Were you in the operating room?" I asked.

"Yes."

"No wonder. Didn't Mother Superior warn you about that room?"

"No."

An Indian who cries and goes into the operating room—no wonder his mother doesn't come to see him! I thought. *I better stick around and get this kid straightened out.*

"Can you sit up?" I asked.

"Sure, it only hurts when I cough."

"Better not do that when the doctors are around."

Bobby asked me if I played checkers. I told him sure, and so we began to play. About ten games later, the little nun walked in and asked how things were going. Bobby said everything was all right and that he wanted to go downstairs to see my room. She told him that when he got a little better, she would permit it. "However, right now the Mother Superior would like to see Ray," she said. *Uh-oh, now what did I do?* I thought.

When we got to the Mother Superior's room, I knocked on the door and she called me in. There stood the policeman who had brought me to the school. "Remember me?" he asked.

"Sure," I answered.

"I have news for you. Your family had a good Easter dinner, and they are saving up money so they can buy a car and come to pick you up."

"If you see them, tell them I'm all right, and I have another mother to help me."

"Who's the other mother?"

"The Mother Superior, of course."

"Well, if you need anything again, just ask the Mother to call me," the policeman said.

I thanked him. He shook my hand and walked out. After he left I was about to head for my room again, but the Mother Superior asked me if I had cheered up that little boy. "I hope so," I answered.

She asked me if he had stopped crying. "Yes," I reported. "He didn't know that Indian boys are not allowed to cry."

"Do you think that will work?" asked the Mother Superior.

"Sure. And I told him to stay out of the operating room so he won't get hurt again."

She put her hand over her eyes, and I thought I'd better leave or she might get out her handkerchief again.

Mr. Shea returned early in the evening. "All the other boys arrived early, so we must get back quickly," he said. I told him the Mother Superior wanted me to stop by her office before I left. So we went there right away and had a sad good-bye. Her door was always open, just like her heart and mind. Mr. Shea knocked as we entered and asked if I was any bother during my stay. Mother Superior told him that I was no bother at all. In fact, she told him, I was a great help.

After Mr. Shea thanked her, I asked if she would do me one last favor. "Tell Bobby I had to return to school. And tell him to stay away from the operating room."

She watched us as we turned to go. When we got to the door, I ran back to her open arms, and she gave me a big hug and kissed me on the cheek. Mr. Shea came back to take my hand, and I waved as I left.

"She must really like you," Mr. Shea said as we got into the car. "I think she was almost in tears."

"All mothers cry a lot," I told him.

11

Back to Classes

After Easter break, the little nun was still keeping an eye on me. I tried to whisper to Jim that I was sorry about the big fight we'd had, but then the nun yelled out, "Raymond! Stop talking. See me after class."

"Now you're really going to get it," said Jim.

After all the boys left, I sat in my seat and waited for the nun's book to hit me on the head. Instead she motioned me to come up to her desk. She asked me why I was talking in class. I told her that I had wanted to apologize to Jim, and she said, "You could do that after class."

"But," I explained, "I promised the Mother Superior I would do it as soon as I saw him again."

"When did you see the Mother Superior?"

"Yesterday. She took me to church."

"Explain to me why the Mother Superior took you to church."

"Well, everyone left for Easter vacation and I was alone, so Mr. Shea took me to the hospital for all of last week."

"Don't you have a home?"

"Yes, but my mother couldn't pick me up."

"When did you last see your mother?"

"Last Christmas."

"You mean to tell me that no one has come to visit you all this time?"

"That's right. My father died, and my mother couldn't support us because we have no money."

"Where will you go when school closes?"

"The Mother Superior told me to come back to the hospital when vacation starts."

"What else did she tell you?

"She told me not to fight anymore and to explain to you that I was really sick when I stuck out my tongue that day."

"Is that all?"

"No. I promised the man on the cross that I would not smoke and that I'll try to be good from now on."

She slowly turned toward the blackboard and didn't say anything. After a while I got impatient. Then she turned around but didn't look up at me. She simply reached under her habit for her handkerchief. With her head down, I thought she was falling asleep because she made no effort to speak to me. Finally she spoke. "You can go now." As I was about to leave, she added, "I promise to never hit you again with a book in this class."

"Thank you, Sister. The Mother Superior was right."

"About what?"

"She said to ask the man up there on the cross for forgiveness and everything would be all right."

After I stood there in front of her for a moment, she asked me if there was anything else I wanted to know. There was just one more thing.

"Sister, why do women always cry?"

"Because they are women."

The rest of the semester seemed to pass as quickly as the week I had spent at the hospital. Soon everyone seemed to be talking about the annual end-of-the-year picnic to be held at one of the lakes near Keshena.

I wondered if I'd have to stay at the hospital all summer. *Better pray to the man up there for more help*, I told myself.

12

Picnic

The night before the picnic, we could hardly get to sleep as we wondered what to expect once we got to the lake. We had been told about games, boat rides, and swimming, and we daydreamed about the food and prizes. But the picnic meant it was the end of the school year, and I was worried about where I would be placed. Would I go back to the hospital? Or would I go somewhere else? Some boys were sent to orphanages off the reservation.

The next day, two stake-bed trucks pulled up to the dorm before noon, and we piled into them so fast Mr. Shea didn't even get a chance to get seated in the cab. Once he took his seat, I swear the truck sank about two feet.

When we arrived at the lake, we hit the beach like a bunch of Marines, and the fun began. Someone threw a football, and I ran and caught it. Bad move. I was hit from the side and landed on my ass about ten feet away. As I stood up, some guy caught another pass and ran toward me. I was hit so hard he knocked me over, and all three of us were on the ground. That did it! No more football for me.

Volleyball, here I come! We punched that ball back and forth over the net so many times I was getting tired. Then some big kid who was running tripped and hit me so hard, I thought I had gotten hit by Mr. Shea. Enough of that. I decided to go on a boat ride.

Just as I was about to climb into the boat, someone hollered, "Swimming, everyone!" But there was one big problem; none of us had swimming suits. "Just use your birthday suits," said Mr. Shea. I asked him what a birthday suit was.

"Go bare ass!" Jim replied before Mr. Shea could tell me anything further. Well, that I could do, because at home I had no swimming suit and we'd all go bare ass.

We played "Periscope." This meant lying on your back, floating in the water with your external manifestation pointing upwards. This game went on until someone came along, threw a stone, and scored a direct hit on some boy's periscope, and the whole submarine jumped clear out of the water. No more submarines dared to surface after that.

We continued swimming until some dirty dog showed up who had had his mother drive him to the picnic—along with his sisters. Someone yelled, "GIRLS!" When we saw them coming, we dashed for our clothes, not caring whose clothes we grabbed. I wound up with a pair of pants that would have fit Mr. Shea.

Scratched and bruised, we made it back to the picnic area. The tables were loaded with sandwiches, hot dogs, potato salad, cake, and ice cream. To us, this was fit for a king. All we had to do was say a prayer and then we could start eating.

Some kids ate too much and got sick, but not Raymond. I remembered what my mother always said: "Eat just enough to get full and save a little room for ice cream."

The feast went until about four o'clock. Then Mr. Shea told us, "Start getting ready to go back to the dorm. Your parents will be picking you up." I had dreaded this moment. At the tender age of eight and a half, I was already a lone wolf, ostracized from my family because my older brothers wouldn't help my mother support us.

Then I thought of the Good Mother and how nicely she had treated me. I thought about all the nurses and even the little nun. Maybe Bobby was still at the hospital. I hoped not.

No one would know how lonesome I was that day, but I never did cry. Sometimes tears would form, and I would quickly run to the washroom to throw some cold water on my face. Then I would look up to Father Sky and say, "Forgive me, Father, for being so weak." This was the time to show that I was a real Indian, not some weakling. Nevertheless, it was hard to comprehend my deplorable situation.

13

Return to the Reservation

Back at the school, Mr. Shea sat down beside me on the dormitory steps. He asked, "How would you like to spend the summer with me and my family?" I smiled and replied, "I have a little sister at home who depends on me, and I know she'll be upset if I don't come home this summer." I hoped he'd understand. He nodded and smiled.

Soon everyone was gone, and I knew no one was going to pick me up, so I walked into Mr. Shea's office and asked him to take me back to the hospital. He told me to get my things together and wait on the steps. As I waited, I looked toward the main gate and saw a 1929 Model A Ford slowly approaching. It stopped right in front of me, the door opened, and out rushed my eldest sister, Mary. With tears running down her face, she threw her arms around me and kissed me on the cheek. Mary resembled the movie star Ava Gardner but was much more beautiful.

"Why didn't you come back to visit him?" Mr. Shea asked her.

"We were so broke, we barely made a living," Mary answered.

"But it's been almost six months!"

"I know," sighed Mary. "I just got a job, and this is my first payday. Now he won't ever be coming back here!"

Mary took me by the hand, and a man got out of the driver's

side of the car. He introduced himself as Melvin. "I'm going to help your family get back on their feet," he assured me, "and I'm going to marry your sister Cecelia."

After meeting Melvin, I turned to take one last look at the mountain of a man who had taken care of me the past semester. I thanked him for being so kind and for all the consideration he showed me during the winter and spring. He reached down for my hand and shook it. I think I noticed a little moisture forming in his eyes, but that's all right, white men are allowed to cry.

As we were leaving, I waved to him until we got out of the gate and out of sight. Mr. Shea just stood there and kept waving. *We shall meet again . . . it's only a matter of time,* I said to myself. *May the Great Spirit smile on him from time to time.* It was the last time I saw him.

After we passed the main gate, I asked Melvin if he would stop at the hospital. On the way there, I couldn't help noticing the nice interior of Mel's car. The seats folded forward, and it had a stick shift on the floor. Melvin noticed me checking it out and asked me how I liked it. "Fine," I answered. "How much?" He told me, "Thirty bucks."

"That's kinda high for a Model A."

"Yeah, but it has all new tires and a good engine."

"How many miles to the gallon?" I asked.

"Twenty."

"How fast will it go?"

"Fifty, wide open."

Mary wanted to know why I wanted to go to the hospital. "Are you sick?" she asked. I told her that I wanted to thank the Mother Superior for taking care of me during Easter vacation. As I walked up the steps at the hospital entrance, Mary caught up with me and asked if she could come along. She seemed very eager to meet the Mother Superior. When we entered, the Good Mother walked toward us and hollered, "Raymond!" I ran into her wide open arms, and she gave me a big hug. Next, she took a look at my sister and asked, "Who is this young lady?"

"That's my sister Mary," I answered.

"Hi," Mary said, smiling at the Mother Superior. "Ray mentioned you were very nice to him, so I just had to meet you and thank you for being so kind."

"He was no bother," the Good Mother said. "In fact, he helped us many times. Will he be staying with us again?"

"No, I'm taking him home, and he won't be coming back this fall. I have a job now."

What my sister told the Mother Superior next surprised me. She said she wanted to become a nun! The Good Mother told her to finish high school first and then go and talk to the priest in Neopit.

After our visit, we headed back out the entrance door, and I turned to wave good-bye to the Mother Superior. She waved, and I thought I saw her reach for her handkerchief. *That's okay*, I thought, *all mothers cry*.

Soon we were homeward bound. The Model A purred along at about forty miles per hour. I felt like I had just gotten out of prison. This lone wolf has got to be free! No walls to confine me! I looked forward to being among the pines near the Wolf River again. Melvin must have sensed my eagerness. "We'll be there in a little while," he promised. Yet it seemed to take hours.

Finally we pulled into our driveway. It was the happiest

moment of my young life. I opened the door, and my little sister was there to meet me. We grabbed each other's arms and jumped around and around.

"Welcome home," my mother said once we stopped jumping.

My mother then began to tell me how tough they had had it. At times they had no food, and they almost froze to death. I wondered why my brothers didn't provide wood for the stove. Then I realized that they must have been too lazy to cut the wood. "You could have written me about all of this," I complained.

I noticed that my mother was having difficulty answering my questions, and I stopped myself before I could ask any more. I figured it was about time I think of the future and try to forget the past.

Catherine motioned for me to come into the kitchen. She asked, "How about a sandwich?"

To my surprise, the kitchen was packed. There were sweet rolls, cookies, store bread, and some lunch meat in the cooler. Mary had said she had a job, but she hadn't told me where. Later I found out that it was at the general store in town. The Great Spirit had smiled on us, and I made an offering to him for being so kind.

The next time Melvin said he was going into town, I asked if I could go with him. Mary was working at the store, and she was glad to see us. She smiled and asked what we would like. I ordered a candy bar, Cracker Jacks, and an ice cream cone. This all came to fifteen cents. She said I shouldn't worry about the cost. So I surprised her by handing her a dollar bill.

"Where did you get this?" she gasped.

"From Mr. Shea," I replied.

I bought my little sister the same items I had chosen for myself.

Mary warned me, "Don't tell your brothers, or they'll be asking you for cigarettes!"

Once we were back home, my mother thought Mary had bought the candy for us. I told my little sister about our secret bank, all seventy cents of it, and she promised not to say a word about it. Besides, I still had another dollar left. We were rich!

After we ate our candy, my little sister and I headed for the river. We threw stones into the water, and then we got bored and decided to go to the frog pond. When we got there, Catherine screamed and pointed at the ground near her feet. There in the grass was a very large pine snake. It moved toward us. I pushed my sister away from it and told her to get something to hit it with, but she was too scared to move. I found a stick and went back to look for it, but by then it was gone. The snake must have been looking for frogs, and we just happened to be there at the same time. I remembered what my mother always said: "Never kill anything unless you want to eat it." Fried snake was not my favorite snack.

The encounter with the snake proved too much for my sister, so we went back home to play checkers and draw pictures. We hoped our brothers would stay away from us. Catherine seemed uneasy whenever they were around. Then I was told to go out and chop some wood, and our playtime was cut short. This meant I had to go spy out some dead tree, chop it up, and haul it back home. When I got back, Melvin came out and helped me. He asked me why my brothers didn't come out to help. "Because they're too lazy," I told him. He asked nothing more.

My mother was fixing dough for bread, and she told me to make a fire in the kitchen stove. She was also busy making dough for peanut butter cookies. How about that? I lucked out again.

Melvin said he was going to pick up Mary and wanted to know if Catherine and I wanted to ride along. We jumped into the car. When we got to the store, we looked around to see what we could buy. It didn't take long before I found some comic books. Flash Gordon—that was the one for me! My sister found a Little Orphan Annie book and some coloring books. What a life!

14

Summer

The South Wind was here, and that meant summer had arrived. The mayflowers and lilies were back in the bosom of Mother Earth. The flowers are born, they grow to maturity, wilt, wane, dry up, and die. We can only try to comprehend the lessons they attempt to teach us. What makes mankind any different than the flowers? We are here for a little while and then gone forever.

Now that school had ended and summer had begun, it was time for me to appreciate the endless wonders of the cosmos. It was time to walk among the pines, smell the fresh air, and enjoy being free. No one appreciates the outdoors more than an Indian, at least this Indian. When I don't see the trees for a long while, I get lonesome.

On my walk, I first visited the frog pond to see if I could catch a turtle. No luck. So I headed for the pine ridge to see if I could chase a few chipmunks, but those suckers are unfriendly.

The leaves seemed to beckon to me as they swayed with the breeze. The carpet of green made walking easy on this summer day, so I took off my shoes and felt the soft grass beneath my feet. Then I looked up at the blue and thanked Father Sky for this pleasant summer day. The ducks were back. I heard their quacks and a loon somewhere calling for its mate. The swallows at the sand pit proved interesting, and the red-winged blackbirds along the river-bank had nests by now, maybe even some little ones.

With all this summer activity, it was hard to decide where to go and what fun to have. But as I walked away from the frog pond, I saw a few butterflies fluttering around a puddle. The butterflies reminded me of trout, because once I had seen a trout jump out of the water and catch one. Seeing butterflies made me want to go trout fishing.

My favorite fishing hole was about two miles away. To get there I had to walk along Highway 47 to Camp 4 Hill, then turn left and walk along a trail to a dam. Just before the dam, there were springs bubbling up from the ground. It was the best water I have ever tasted.

When I arrived at my fishing hole, I sat on a rock and listened to the rushing water, leaned back, and looked up at the clear blue sky. I decided fishing could wait. I would just lie back and observe the wonders of nature. It made me feel happy to be alive. Everything seemed to be new. Everything, that is, except me; this would be my tenth summer.

The North Wind had bowed to the South Wind, permitting her to come and warm our hearts after the long, cold winter. This is the time of year my mother would make an offering to the Great Spirit for giving us another nice summer.

Eventually I started fishing. I caught two trout, but the fish seemed to stop biting so I decided to head for home. Remembering the Indian Way, I would go back with just enough fish to eat. Two trout were enough for me and my little sister.

When I started to leave, I noticed something I had never seen before: bear droppings! I knew I better get going fast. Bears like fish, and if I encountered one, I'd have to throw my trout at her. Most animals give birth to their young in the spring, and spring is when the animal mothers get mean. This includes bears and wolves, too. All summer I wouldn't go back to my favorite fishing hole for fear of that old bear. She might invite me to dinner and have me as her main dish! I wished I had a dog to help me.

My mother took the trout I brought home and began to prepare them for my first trout dinner since last year. "Don't go too far away. Supper will be ready in a few moments," she called to me as I headed back outside.

Walking among the huge pines, I looked up to see their crests bending with the wind, as if they were welcoming me back. Those trees were there long before I was born. They are still there today, and I know they will be there long after I'm gone.

Next time you're near a pine tree, remember this: it's a living thing just like you and me. The tree needs water and nutrients to live and has old Father Sky to pray to every day. Take a good look at a tree and see its limbs. They're pointed upwards, as if in prayer. When you're feeling lonely, get up close to a pine tree, sit in its shade, look up at Father Sky, and be grateful you are alive. Soon you'll realize that you're only here for a little while and that the tree you're sitting next to will be here long after you're gone.

I watched the birds fluttering near the tops of the trees, and they seemed to be in a hurry to get somewhere. Then I noticed dark clouds forming, and the next big gust of wind sent me heading for home. Summer is the time the trees get washed and Mother Earth makes everything fresh again. The rain does many things to the soil as well, and without it our garden would not produce so many delectable plants that nourish our bodies. What would we do without rain? Yet when the rain comes down for too long, we hope it stops. Remember the Indian Way: hope for just enough, not too much.

That summer of 1934 seemed to be passing quickly. Soon my mother started talking about going to Sturgeon Bay, a city located north of Green Bay. When I asked why we were going there, my mother told me, "It's cherry-picking time."

15

Cherry-Picking Time

Cherry-picking time was an annual event lasting about two weeks in July. The people who owned the farms in the area would send out trucks to transport workers back and forth from the cherry orchards. When the trucks arrived in our town, we were ready. Off we'd go, headed for Sturgeon Bay.

When we passed Green Bay, I spotted the biggest body of water I had ever seen. My mother told me that it was Green Bay, adding, "They call the bay that because it appears to be green." That made sense to me.

Once we got to Sturgeon Bay, I wondered what a sturgeon looked like, because Sturgeon Bay must have gotten its name from the fish. Years later I found out that once there had indeed been a lot of sturgeons in those waters.

When we reached the cherry orchards, we could see the trees were loaded with fruit, and when we passed under one we could grab a handful. The owners of the orchard had living quarters set up for us, and all we had to do was put clean sheets on the beds. My mother had brought along blankets and clothing for us.

We were given cards to be punched every time we turned in a full bucket of cherries. We earned three cents a bucket. At the end of the day I had ten holes punched into my card and was given thirty cents, all in nickels. Hey, I was rich again!

Then there was more good news. Near the barn, a collie had given birth to puppies. Remembering about mothers and their offspring, I asked the owner of the farm if the mother collie was friendly. "Sure," he said, "just call her Queenie, and pet her first." Before I attempted to make friends with Queenie, I ran back to the living area and found some food scraps. When I walked up to Queenie, she wagged her tail, and then I knew she was friendly. I gave her the tidbits, and henceforth she always wagged her tail when she saw me coming. One day the owner noticed this and said, "She really likes you."

I said, "She must know that I would like to have one of her pups."

About a week later, while I was playing with the pups, the farmer told me that he was going to sell them. I pointed to a little male puppy that I liked, and I got lucky again.

"It's yours," the farmer said.

I ran to tell my mother I had a puppy to take home with us. She gave me a serious look and said, "Ray, that dog will never survive the cold winter. Only wolves can survive in thirty-below temperatures." She was right. Why do mothers always have to be right?

But good news was coming my way again. A truck was going into town for the movies. I wanted to take my little sister to her first movie. She was excited and could hardly wait for the truck. I hoped that this time the movie would not be the Marx Brothers. The movie cost five cents, and it was another five cents for popcorn and a bottle of Coke. The popcorn was in a paper bag, and when they poured butter on top of it, some of it soaked right through the paper. The Coke came in a small bottle with a straw. Candy bars were five cents, and some of them were frozen.

The theaters back in those days always featured a double movie. The first we saw was about airplanes, and the other one was a gangster movie with James Cagney. Every time a gun was fired, my little sister would jump. She liked the airplane movie much better. When the movies were over, we were eager to tell our mother all the exciting news. But she had never been to a movie in her entire life and wasn't all that interested in hearing about them.

The cherry harvest lasted only about two weeks, and I was not looking forward to going back home. The whole family was sorry to leave our living quarters, and already we looked forward to the next cherry season. While we were packing, my mother told me, "The potato harvest is next, remember?" Maybe we'd be able to make more money!

I asked my mother one last time if I could have the puppy. I told her that I would keep him inside when it got cold. She put a hand on my shoulder and said, "Ray, a dog's place is outside. Besides, when it starts to shed its fur we'd have hair all over the house." She was right again.

That night I dreamed of a wolf. When I told my mother about the dream, she just smiled and said, "Oh, you have wolves on your mind. No wonder—there was a wolf howling last night." The news startled me. Some Indians believe that when a person dies, he returns as a wolf.

16

First Driving Lesson

July 25, 1934, was my tenth birthday, and I was given a small teddy bear. (I treasured that little bear for years, but I lost it when I finally left home. Now I have another one enclosed in a glass container. I look at it from time to time and reminisce about my tenth birthday and my first teddy bear.) Not long after my birthday, my sister Cecelia was to be married to Melvin.

As preparations for the big event began, Cecelia and Melvin asked me if I wanted to participate in the wedding. "Why not?" I replied. Melvin smiled. We headed out for Shawano to buy wedding presents and the marriage certificate. On the way back home, Mel said to me, "You just had your tenth birthday; now you should start learning how to drive."

With a big smile, I replied, "Okay with me!"

He pulled the seat forward and put his coat over it so that I could see over the hood and reach the pedals. His instructions were explicit:

Steering wheel: turn it left, you go left; turn it right, you go right.

Foot pedals: the one on the left is the clutch; the one on the right is the brake.

Small pedal is the gas pedal.

Shift lever: three speeds forward and one reverse; H pattern—
he showed me the positions.

Here we go! I pushed in the clutch pedal, shifted to the lowest
gear, and released the clutch, slowly. After we started moving, I
shifted to the number two position and then to the number three
position. "Keep driving in the right lane, and never drive on the left
side. You're doing fine," Melvin told me. When he told me to stop,
I stopped. After repeating his instructions, he warned, "Anytime I
catch you driving over the center line, you're going to get a kick in
the ass." Then, more seriously, he added, "Don't tell your mother."

17

Harvest Feast

When you're young, the summer passes too quickly. Although I did not have to go back to the boys' school at Keshena, the thought of going back to school still saddened me, because I would have to wear shoes. New shoes are always hard to break in, especially when you have been going barefoot all summer. The soles of your feet become hard and calloused, making it even more difficult to keep your shoes on.

September began to cool Neopit, with a hint of frost to start the leaves fading and taking on different colors: dark red for maple, yellow for poplar, lighter red for oak, elm a yellow-orange. Mother Earth mixed all these colors together and put on a spectacular show. Walking through the trees, I could smell the aroma of the leaves. It made me want to walk farther. I could walk a mile among those colors and not get tired, the air was so invigorating.

When the geese began to fly south, we knew it was time again to prepare for the long winter months. The white men have Thanksgiving, but not the Indians. How can we be thankful for all the treaties they broke? Better we partake in the Harvest Feast, when we give thanks to the Great Spirit for being so kind to us all summer and for giving us plenty of food for the winter. (Remember that not all Menominee families think and act like my family did. Some participate in celebrating Thanksgiving and Christmas holidays.)

Catholics observe a time they call All Soul's Day, and our family had a version of that, except my mother did things differently. She prepared a huge meal. Then, just as I was about to sit down and satisfy my hunger, she told us to vacate the room and closed all the doors. We had to wait a few minutes before reentering the room. This was the time when the spirits of our ancestors would be invited to partake in the meal, a sign of our appreciation. When I grew older, I noticed that my family was not the only one that did this. Other Menominee families had a similar practice and gave similar offerings.

There is no such thing as an official Indian prayer. This was something my mother taught me. She said, "Talk to the Great Spirit as if he were standing right next to you. Ask for a special favor. Don't pray for one." Outside our house, facing North, my mother would make the following offering:

A Talk with the North Wind—The Kaquatosh Way

Autumn is the time to offer smoke from the Peace Pipe to the North Wind, who brings us the icy winds and covers the Earth with a blanket of white. Long before the water turns to ice, we ask the mighty North Wind to be kind to us during the winter months. Also, we ask the North Wind not to stay any longer than necessary to kill all the germs that cover the Earth. Don't breathe too long on the animals, or they will feel your wrath, for you, O North Wind, are most powerful of all winds. We will talk to you again when you make the water solid like a rock. When you speak to us with your strong voice, make it brief because we know how powerful you are.

We are weak and only here for a little while, but you go on forever. Be kind to us, O Winter Wind, and we will be grateful. Next year we hope to welcome you back, if the Great Spirit permits us.

The humble words of my mother's offering, words spoken to the North Wind, will be with me for a long time. These words may differ slightly from what my mother said, but it is the spirit of the talk with the North Wind that I most remember.

18

Witchcraft

Many ethnic groups practice some sort of rituals considered witchcraft. Some Menominee people practice witchcraft. It is still being used at this time, but all of my witchcraft experiences were during my youth.

I lived two blocks from the cemetery in Neopit, in an area referred to as the Crow's Nest. My home was located on a witch's trail, and I frequently observed witches on their way to do their errands. The term *witch* refers to a female, and a male is called a *wizard,* but because of the lack of understanding in the white man's language, the word *witch* is often used for both.

When I saw a witch on its mission, it was usually in the form of an animal or bird and had a ball of fire in its mouth. The ball of fire itself was not harmful, but it is believed that when one encounters a witch, four days later someone will die.

Taking on the form of an animal is an evil practice done by self-hypnosis. Some people refer to this as shape-shifting. I once watched a man perform this ritual lying flat on the floor with only a blanket for a cushion. He didn't seem to be breathing, and I thought he was dead. He remained in that position until the next morning. When he awakened, he was bruised and had a visible wound on his right arm, possibly caused by an encounter with a person or animal during his ill-fated mission. My mother scolded me for observing his actions.

Some Menominee believe that the soul of a victim of witchcraft must be protected for four days after death. Years ago, a person's body was kept in the home for four days, and someone had to guard the body so that the soul would not be disturbed on its journey to the hereafter.

I'm going to tell you a true story about my Uncle Arthur from Chicago. It happened one night when I was a boy and he was vacationing with us. (My Uncle Arthur was not an Indian.)

Late one evening, when we were all in bed, our room unexpectedly became illuminated to the point that we could see each other clearly. My brother informed me that the light was actually a witch. Uncle Arthur scoffed at this: "There's no such thing as a witch."

The next morning, he packed up everything and returned to Chicago with his family. Once back at home, he went into the bathroom of their apartment, and he never emerged. He was never heard from again.

19

Wolf

Soon the cold first month of 1935 was upon us. The temperature seemed to continually linger below zero, and in this frigid weather I had to walk to school every day. The snow crunched with every step, and my nose turned red. The air was hard to breathe.

One evening I had to make an appearance for a school play that didn't start until after dark. A light snow had fallen earlier that day. As I headed back home and the lights faded behind me, I felt uneasy, like I was being stalked. I was startled when I heard a noise alongside of me. It was so dark I couldn't see my hand in front of my nose, and I didn't know what it was that walked beside me. If we were ever caught in the presence of a wild or dangerous animal, we were told to make a lot of noise. I began to holler and shout, hoping someone nearby would hear me.

It was then that I heard Maggie Lyons's dog bark. I was less afraid of that mean bulldog than of whatever else was out there, and I ran all the way to Maggie's driveway and began to shout for Maggie. She came out of the house, and I told her what had frightened me. She promised to stay by the roadside until I got almost home. She'll never know how much I appreciated that.

When I told my story to my brothers, they laughed and called me a weakling for being afraid of the dark. But later I found some large footprints in the snow. The prints seemed to be like a dog's, but the dog had to be much heavier than your average dog, because the prints sank deep into the snow. After that night I dropped out of the school play, and I decided to carry a knife and a pointed stick with a sharp end—you could call it a lance.

Another snowfall came, and the next morning I was glad to see the blanket of white the North Wind had sent us. With the thick snow, I could build a snow house or a fort to help ward off an imaginary enemy. As I put on my snowshoes, I thought of using the fresh snow to track rabbits, squirrels, and porcupines. Then I thought: *Wolves, too.* I better have my lance ready.

My mother told me that wolves travel in packs because they cannot survive alone. But I wondered if the creature who had come upon me the other night was a lone wolf. That must've been what he was—just a lone wolf. He might have been ostracized from the pack, just like I was when my family sent me to the Keshena boys' school. Hey, we had something in common. I learned that most lone wolves were males, so he had to be a male. And I knew he had followed me that night. Why didn't he attack? He had an easy prey. Later I decided the lone wolf must have been trying to be friendly. I had always wanted a dog; now I realized that the Great Spirit must have sent this animal to me.

Early one morning, as I was getting ready to go to school, my mother told me that the snow was too deep and the plows hadn't had a chance to clear the road, so I had to stay home. Gazing at the pines with their branches heavily laden with snow, I saw the snow suddenly fall from them and the branches quickly swing back up. Then I saw him. He leapt high to get over the heavy snow and look toward our home. Both his ears were pointing straight up. One turned sideways, then forward. Then the other did the same. This indicated to me that his defense mechanisms were functioning. His nose sniffed at the air, and his tail wrapped around his legs. His coat was as almost as white as the snow. What a magnificent sight! I will always remember him like that.

By the time I called my mother to the window, he was gone. She laughed and said, "You got wolves on your mind." Then I thought about the snow. I could find his tracks and prove I was not seeing things. But the tracks would just as easily prove he was a large dog. I knew he was a wolf, but no one would believe me. So there was only one thing to do: kill him before he killed me.

My cousin had a .22-caliber rifle that he allowed me to borrow for the deplorable act I was about to commit. He said, "I hope you get him."

Now all I had to do was wait. It didn't take long.

One bright, sunny morning, the lone wolf returned. When I saw him, about two hundred yards from the house, I rushed to get the rifle and loaded it with the .22 long-range bullet. Slowly, I opened the window and took careful aim at him as he sat peacefully in the snow. Then I squeezed the trigger. BANG! I felt the recoil from the rifle and saw the disturbance of the snow to the left of him. I had missed—because of the wind, or possibly because of divine intervention. I preferred to think it was the latter. I thought I would never get another shot at him. Wolves know when they're being hunted. At least I had scared him off.

My eldest brother woke up when he heard the shot and came rushing downstairs. "What's all the shooting about?" When I told him that I had tried to shoot a wolf, he screamed at me, "That wolf may be one of our relatives who died and came back as a wolf!"

I hadn't considered that I could have killed my own father. The wolf was young and must have been born about the same time my father had died. As I sat by the window with my head hanging down, I felt a hand on my shoulder and looked up to see my mother smiling. "You missed for some good reason. You'll find out later."

For the next few days I couldn't get over the sinful act I had almost committed. It haunted me, and I wished to make amends. The temperature was still below zero, and I didn't have to go to school—nothing to do but keep the home fires burning. One day I took off toward the island on the Wolf River to get firewood. As I crossed the highway, I couldn't help thinking about the lone wolf. I was sure he'd never return. On the way back, I glanced toward the edge of the woods by our home. I thought I saw some movement. Then I saw the wolf jump over a pile of snow. His breath came out in puffs of steam as he ran. He stopped and looked back at me. I froze. Now it was his turn to kill.

When you're facing death, there's only one thing to do: ask the Creator for forgiveness. Just like the Mother Superior said, ask the man upstairs for help, and everything will be all right.

The lone wolf started to walk slowly toward me. He had his head down, and I knew he was about to attack. I was carrying a small tree, and I slowly put it down to grab my axe. Then I looked up at Father Sky and thought, *Oh, Great Spirit, help me befriend this animal I tried to kill. I will never try to harm him again.* At that instant, the wolf stopped walking and sat down.

He let me go.

Slowly, I picked up the tree and started to walk back to the house, keeping an eye on him for any sudden moment. The wolf just sat there, never moving until I got into the house. I ran to tell my mother, "He's back!" I pointed to show her where he was, but by then he was gone.

A little later my mother said a strange thing: "He'll be back. Just don't try to kill him."

She said another strange thing: "Be nice to him."

How can I be nice to a wild animal? Then it occurred to me—food!

That's it. He must be hungry. I would put out some food for him, and maybe this would make up for my trying to shoot him. With below-zero temperatures, it must be difficult to catch something to eat. All the small animals were staying holed up to keep warm. So I put some food around the places I had last seen the wolf, but the wind blew snow over it. Then I got a brilliant idea: I would put some meat on a stick. That way the snow would not cover it. Hey, this little Indian was getting some smarts!

Early one morning, I checked the places I had baited with food. The wolf had taken all the pieces I had put out for him. Now all I had to do was put out more food. Each day I placed the meat closer to the house, and one day I put it in a dish by the door. He didn't mind, and now he had his own dish.

All those years I had yearned for a German shepherd, and now I had something better: an animal that could stay out all winter and not freeze to death. And I didn't even have to build him a doghouse!

One day I put some meat in his dish and waited for him to approach the house. It took a little while, but soon he came running. He stopped when I opened the door. It was the second time I had made eye contact with him. I feared he might take this as a challenge, but I guess he was too hungry. The next day I threw some meat at him, and he ran away. Maybe he thought I was angry at him.

Each morning about the same time, I put some food in his dish. One morning he was waiting, and as I approached him, he wagged his tail. *Hey, this guy's getting friendly!* I thought. Now all I had to do was talk to him or whistle. Every time I put out food, I would whistle or bang on a pan, and he'd come running. Any sudden move, and he'd run away. I'd slowly walk over close to him to fill his dish, then slowly walk away.

Next, a bigger test. After giving him his food one day, I took my axe and headed for his domain. Sure enough, he started tailing me and waited while I chopped down a tree. He followed me home and then returned to the woods.

I was still afraid to walk to school, so I always took my lance and my jackknife with me. Now on the way to school, Catherine and I would see the wolf running along the highway. When we got to the playground, he disappeared back into the woods.

One day while I was at school, I suddenly remembered that I had forgotten to put out food for the wolf. *Oh, well, he won't starve,* I thought. *I'll put some out later.*

When I entered the house, my mother was shaken up. She told me, "I was outside, and that wolf jumped on my arm!" Still shaking, she added, "I thought he was going to attack, and I screamed." I told her I had forgotten to put out some food for him, and he was just being friendly.

"Now you tell me," she grumbled.

The lone wolf didn't return for two days, and I thought I had lost him. He kept out of sight, and I thought it was a waste of time to go look for him because he was too frightened to return. Nevertheless, I kept putting food in his dish, and one day he returned and took all of it. Now all I had to do was regain his confidence.

It didn't take long. After I called him for his daily meal and he had his fill, I decided to walk along the riverbanks to gather firewood. He followed and ran ahead of me, then turned and ran close by my side. As he ran close to me again, I brushed his back. He kept doing this and wagged his tail. Then he slowed down so I could brush his back. I even petted his head. His bushy tail just kept wagging. Once again he trusted me, and I would not let him down again, ever.

He was a timber wolf, just like the one my father encountered on his way home from the logging camps. He must have been about a year and a half old. He seemed to be fully grown and weighed about seventy-five pounds. As he grew older, he put on more weight and grew taller.

Everyone said to me, "You cannot tame a wolf." We showed them! I also had to get him to accept the others in my family. That took a little more time, but we had a lot of that. I had a wolf, and the wolf had me.

20

Kernel

It was hard to believe this magnificent animal was my friend. He embodied the Indian spirit of freedom—he roamed the territory and also displayed aloofness. We had something else in common: we were both lone wolves. The only friends I had were my little sister and my wolf.

Now I had to think of a name for him. Corn to the Indian is like bread to the white man—"the staff of life." When the seed of corn is planted and combines with the Earth, it starts to grow. This wolf was a seed of friendship, so I called him Kernel. My brothers approved of the name because they thought I had called him Colonel, like in the Army. I never told them that I had the seed in mind when I named him.

At first when I called his name, he just looked at me. So whenever I put food in his dish, I would say his name. Then every time I wanted his attention, I'd holler his name. It didn't take too long for him to respond.

One day I put a loose rope around Kernel's neck, and it almost cost me our friendship. Kernel tried to bite it off and tried to bite me also. I quickly slipped it off and petted him for a long time after. He had lived his whole life without a collar. He had to be free just like me. Putting a collar around that wolf's neck was a dumb thing to do.

———

"When life is progressing well, beware of the unexpected," my mother always reminded me. One day when we started back home from school, some boys were waiting for us along the way. They turned their dogs loose, and the dogs attacked Kernel. I thought they were going to tear him apart! With my heavy winter clothing and gloves on, I grabbed one of the dogs by the tail and pulled it off Kernel. It didn't take long for Kernel to send the other dog squealing down the road, but the one I had by the tail turned on me and bit into my coat. The dog had me by the arm and would not let go. The boys were laughing at us as the dog dragged me along. Kernel chased the dog that ran off, but soon he came running back to see the other dog biting my arm. Kernel bit that dog on the neck and started dragging it backwards, with my arm still in the dog's mouth. Finally I managed to break loose.

Kernel and the dog stood on their hind legs, looking almost like boxers, trying to get an opening for a knockout punch. Then Kernel got the dog by the throat and ripped part of it out. When the blood started to pour out of the dog, it could no longer stand and soon it fell over and died. I turned to those other boys and said, "You sons of bitches, I hope you had a good laugh."

"Your wolf killed my dog!" one protested.

"Why didn't you just call him off me?" I replied.

"Oh, he was just playing."

"You're a lying son of a bitch. Look at my arm!" I showed him where his dog bit into me.

"So he nipped you."

"Look at my arm! It's bleeding. That's a nip?"

"We should have never done this," said the other boy.

"Yeah," I huffed, "tell that to that dead dog over there!"

This was the first time Kernel displayed ferocity toward another dog. He usually backed away. But this was not his fault. He did what was best for both of us. Now we had to go home and lick our wounds. My arm was bleeding, yet I felt sorry for that dead dog.

Kernel looked like he was bleeding, so I hurried home to check his wounds. When I wiped his coat, I found that most of the blood was from the other dog. I tried to examine him further, but he just shook his coat, letting me know that he was all right.

When we got home, my arm was still bleeding, and my mother said, "We better get you to a doctor." She added, "I suppose the police will be making a visit soon." She was right again. When we were getting ready to head for town, there was a knock at the door. My mother answered, "Come in!" and in came the town policeman. "I came to shoot your wolf," he said.

With a stern look, my mother told him, "You'll have to shoot my son, also."

"Why?" asked the policeman.

"He was being mauled by one of those boys' dogs, and his wolf killed it. Is that a good enough reason to kill it?"

The policeman took off his cap and scratched his head. "I guess not," he said. Then he asked if I would tell him about it.

I told him everything. When I finished, the policeman asked why the two boys didn't stop their dogs. I told him that the boys thought it was funny. "Well, I don't think it's funny, and that is not what they told me," replied the policeman.

I hugged Kernel close and asked, "You're not going to shoot him?"

"No," sighed the policeman, "but don't take him into town, or someone else might."

The policeman seemed to be convinced by my story, and he gave me a ride to the doctor's office. He told me once I got patched up I should come to the station. "What for?" I asked, and he said, "I want to get those two boys straightened out."

After taking care of my wounds, a kindly doctor told me to come back in two days.

We went to see the man who made the complaint about the dead dog. He let us in and asked why we were there. The policeman answered, "To explain why your dog got killed." He told me to tell the man what happened. The man had a mean look on his face, but I looked at him and repeated what I had told the policeman. "Your dog had me on the ground with my arm in its mouth, and it was dragging me around, and your son did nothing to stop it," I added. "He just stood there laughing. That's when my wolf attacked."

The man turned to his son. "Is that true?"

His son didn't answer. He just turned away and looked down at the floor. He wouldn't look at me or the policeman. "Answer me, Mike!" his father demanded. The kid started to cry. What a disgrace, an Indian boy who cries.

The policeman told Mike he owed me an apology. His father refuted, "He doesn't owe anyone anything." When the policeman asked if I wanted to file a complaint about the incident, I shook my head no.

As we were about to leave, I said to Mike, "When my arm heals, I wanna have a little talk with you."

"Then I will have a talk with you!" Mike's dad snapped.

The policeman gave a hard look at the man and replied, "Then I will have a talk with you, understand?" The man didn't answer.

On the way home, the policeman told me that he never did like that guy. "Now I've lost all respect for him."

When my mother found out who the man was, she asked what was going to be done about my arm. The policeman told her that I had refused to make a complaint, but it wasn't too late to make one. "That guy is a sneaky, lying, low-down skunk," my mother spat. They both laughed. I didn't smile. My arm was still hurting.

Kernel's wounds healed quickly, and he never showed signs of discomfort. All he did was roll in the snow, and his coat was clean of all the blood stains. At night he returned to the woods to sleep. He never had need for me to make him a doghouse. He made his own under a big fallen tree.

One day I accidentally found it. He had dug under the tree and bedded the ground with leaves. It looked pretty comfortable to me. This was his den, and he used it only when weather permitted. When it got to twenty or thirty below, he would dig a hole in the snow. In the morning, I'd call him, and he'd break through the snow, shaking his coat as he came out, ready for action.

Every morning when I was about to depart for school, I told Kernel to stay home. After the dog attack, it was difficult to make him stay. He seemed to sense that I needed protection, but it was really the other way around. He needed to be protected from people.

21

Another Fight

After Kernel killed the dog, he watched after me carefully, and he'd growl if any dog got near me. This protective front made me feel like I was king of the hill, but it reminded that I'd better keep Kernel away from Maggie Lyons's bulldog.

Maggie, who lived halfway between school and my home, had a real mean bulldog that looked like a small tiger, light brown with black stripes. If that dog tangled with a buzz saw, I bet he would have come out the victor. He had jaws any shark would be proud of. He ruled the road by Maggie's house, and most people would avoid the area. But I had to pass by her house every day. Every time the bulldog saw me approach, he would chase me for a little ways and then return home with a triumphant gait. He was king of the territory, and he knew it.

Maggie would always say, "Oh, he won't bite," but she would laugh when that S.O.B. chased me down the road. This had gone on for about a year. Now it was about the middle of February, and Kernel was all healed up from his fight with the other dogs. He seemed to have put on a few pounds, but at times I noticed he had cuts or bite marks on his legs, and I couldn't figure out why. Then one day I realized that he had been mauled by the little bulldog.

Kernel had a built-in timer, and when three o'clock rolled

around he would get restless and try to get out of the woodshed. One day he was waiting for me after school, and he greeted me with his bushy tail wagging. I wondered how he got by Maggie's house. *Her dog must have taken the day off,* I thought. Now we would somehow have to get past her driveway on the way back.

When we were in front of the driveway, I saw the dog running toward us, so I motioned to Kernel to get going. He obeyed and ran ahead of me. Hoping to get past without incident, all I could do was run. The bulldog caught up with me and got me by the leg.

Kernel turned to see that I was in trouble. By this time, I was on the ground trying to kick the dog loose from my leg. Kernel jumped right over me and nailed that dog on the back of the neck, tore him loose from my leg, and threw him into the air. Now the fight between them really began.

The bulldog was bleeding badly from the wound on his neck, but he was not about to give up. Kernel got him by the neck again and shook him like a ragdoll. I watched, helpless to stop it. The bulldog got a good grip on Kernel's hind leg. Now what? Only one thing to do. I cheered Kernel on. I began to holler, "Get him, Kernel! Come on, Kernel, get him!"

This was the turning point. Kernel tore some flesh from the bulldog's neck. The bulldog grew weak but still would not let loose. "Get him!" I hollered some more, and each time I hollered, Kernel would tear off more flesh. Finally the dog let go of Kernel's leg and fell over, dead. Now what?

I checked to see how badly Kernel was hurt. He wagged his tail and went back to take another bite out of that dog, as if to make sure he had killed it.

When we got home, my mother packed snow on Kernel's leg

to make sure his bleeding stopped. Now we would have to face up to its owner.

I ran halfway to the police station, hoping that the same policeman who helped me before would be there. I lucked out. He noticed me and asked, "Those boys bothering you again?" I told him it was something worse.

"Maggie's bulldog," I said.

He looked at the ceiling and replied, "We've had a lot of complaints about that dog. Someday I'm going to have to shoot it."

"You won't have to now."

"Why?" he asked.

"Because my wolf just killed it."

He smiled and thanked me and my wolf. Then I showed him the bottom of my trousers where the bulldog had torn into my leg. The policeman was still smiling when he said, "That dog turned on me once, and Maggie did nothing to stop it."

When Maggie found out about her dog, she came over to my house and started yelling at my mother. When she found out her dog started the fight, she seemed to back down a little. My mother showed her my torn trousers. Maggie said she was sorry and walked out.

Now it was my turn to be protective. In order to keep Kernel safe, I could not permit him to wander away from home. I couldn't leave him alone for too long, either. Who would have ever thought a wolf needed so much protection? I had to put out signs near our home: TAME WOLF—DON'T SHOOT!

I also had to tell people in town about Kernel. The people I told looked at me like I was a little loco, and some just laughed.

Next I had to train Kernel to say away from the road. This took some time, but he was a good learner.

While I took measures to protect him, I thought about the time I had tried to shoot him. How could I teach him to be afraid of guns? People shoot things from their cars and don't care what they shoot. I hoped they'd see my signs. We were getting along just fine, and everything seemed to be in our favor, if only people would leave us alone.

———

Kernel's keen hunting skills were extraordinary. When we went out hunting for partridges, he would stop when he spotted one, staring at a tree without moving. Following his gaze, I would spot the bird, take careful aim, and shoot it. When it fell to the ground, Kernel would run to pick it up and return it to me with a wagging tail.

It didn't take him long to track down a rabbit. All I had to do was point to a rabbit trail and tell him, "Go get 'em!" When I heard him bark, I knew a rabbit was on its way toward me. All I had to do was wait.

One day we were hunting, and I told him "Go!" He looked at me and then headed for the woods. He didn't return for some time, and I started to get impatient. Then, as I was about to walk away, he came running with a rabbit in his mouth and dropped it at my feet, his tail wagging. I bent down and gave him a hearty hug. He licked my face and jumped on my arm as we rushed home.

When I told my mother what he had done, she looked at the rabbit and said, "Give him the whole thing." So I filled his dish and watched him eat. Then I noticed a small piece he left behind.

He looked at me, then looked back at his dish. Would you believe he left that portion for me? So I made believe I ate it, and later I gave it to him. What an animal!

"When things are going smoothly, beware!" my mother always told me. She was right. Here's what happened next.

22

Tragedy

Late in February the weather turned bitter cold, and the schools were closed. We needed firewood. With an axe on my shoulder, I crossed the highway, turned to see if Kernel was following me, and noticed that he was nowhere in sight. A car passed by, and a moment later I heard a BANG! I knew someone had fired a gun from the road. I ran toward the car. A man stood near his car, his rifle still pointed at the side of the road.

I hollered, "Wait! What are you shooting at?"

"A wolf," he replied.

This can't be happening to my wolf, I thought. The man pointed in the direction where Kernel must have been. I started running and soon saw a trail of blood. I knew he was hit, but I hoped it would be a minor injury. I found him still sitting up, and he recognized me, a good sign. After wrapping my coat around him, I ran back to the man who shot him. "Help me get him home!" I pleaded. We carried Kernel home and put him in the woodshed. I made a bed for him, and my mother packed his wound with snow to stop the bleeding.

I turned to the man who shot Kernel and said, "Didn't you see the signs I put out?" He shook his head no. I then asked him, "You know Mike's father?" He just hung his head and didn't answer.

"If that wolf dies, someone in your family will die, too!" my mother warned him. He never said another word. He just walked back to his car.

After the man left, we moved Kernel inside. As I held the snow packs my mother prepared, she began to cry. She knew Kernel was badly wounded, but I didn't give up hope.

All that night he lay there, motionless, and I just watched his breathing and prayed that each one wouldn't be his last. When the bleeding stopped, we put a Vaseline-soaked cloth on his wound. Now we had to wait and hope no infection would set in. Each time we changed the bandages, there were fewer signs of blood, and soon there was none, a good sign. I kept telling myself that he couldn't die and that I had to do something, but what? I dozed off. When I woke I noticed that his breathing had returned to normal.

The East Wind began to chase away the darkness. The sky brightened and the clouds were red. It was then I knew the Great Breath-Maker would let Kernel live another day. My mother put her hand on my shoulder and said, "The bleeding has stopped, and now all he needs is a lot of rest."

"Will he make it?" I asked.

"Wolves are tougher than dogs and are hard to kill."

I hung my head low and said, "I know. I tried to shoot him once."

My mother gave me a dark glance. "You better have a talk with the Breath-Maker, or he'll never make it."

As I brushed his head, I promised, "From now on I'll be more careful, and I'll not let this happen again." Kernel licked his chops, and I knew he was thirsty. I poured a little water on his tongue and kept doing this until he'd had enough. Another good sign.

"He's getting better," my mother said.

All day I watched for his tongue and kept giving him water. There was no sign of infection, yet he still couldn't lift his head, so I just had to wait for further signs of improvement. The second day was the same as the first, except he was getting thirstier. On the third day, I saw him try to lift his head and so, slowly, I lifted his head a bit more. To my surprise, he started to lick the water. Now I had to get some food in him. Chicken noodle soup—that was his favorite. I rushed to the store and bought him three cans. As he lay motionless, I put a pillow under his head and said to my mother, "He must be in a lot of pain. I can't let him suffer any longer."

Just as I turned toward the door, my mother said, "Look, his tail just wagged!"

I turned back to see the most beautiful sight I could imagine. That old bushy tail flopped up and down. I opened one of the cans and warmed up the soup. Then I carefully lifted his head and watched in amazement as he slowly lapped up the whole dish of soup. After he was done, I lowered his head, and his tail flopped a couple times as if to say thanks. I petted his head as he closed his eyes. I sat there with tears streaming down my cheeks, and I didn't care if the whole world saw them.

Kernel was getting better each day, and I could see his strength returning. At times he tried to sit up. One day I helped him. There he sat, and we looked at each other. "You made it," I told him. My mother must have been watching, because she handed me a little hamburger and replied, "See if he can eat this now." I gave it to him, and to my surprise he ate most of it. Now for some rest. As he fell asleep, I stroked his head. The Breath-Maker had heard my plea.

Kernel's wound consisted of a tear beneath his front leg. He must have been facing the gunman. The bullet had entered from the front and went clear through him. His leg muscles were not damaged too badly. He limped for a while but seemed to heal a lot faster after limping around.

The policeman heard about this, and one day he stopped to tell me that the man who shot my wolf was in the hospital. I asked what happened to him. The policeman reported, "He was impaled by a sharp end of a board under his right arm." This was the same area where my wolf had been hit.

I smiled and said, "Well, that's what he gets for shooting my wolf."

The policeman asked how Kernel was getting along. I told him that he was getting better every day. He walked back toward his squad car, then stopped, turned, and said, "You take good care of him."

Smiling, I assured him that Kernel was the one who took care of me. "He helps me hunt rabbits and partridges. And we even go fishing together," I said.

The policeman shook his head and waved as he left.

I knew the Great Breath-Maker had spared Kernel for me. Now I had to show my gratefulness by making some kind of offering. As I looked up at Father Sky, I said, "Thank you, Great Breath-Maker! Someday my Kernel will make you proud of him."

23

Boy and Wolf

They say there's no prettier picture than a boy and his dog. But there is one better: a boy and his wolf. Or is it a wolf and his boy?

I spent the rest of that winter conditioning Kernel. People told me you cannot teach a wolf to do tricks like you can a dog. I disagreed. How do you condition a wolf? Easy: be repetitious, be rewarding, and always be in command. It took time, but we had a lot of that.

While he was sitting, I gently took Kernel's paw and scratched it. Each time I did this, I would say, "Shake." Then I'd give him a tidbit. He seemed to like getting his paw rubbed or scratched. Soon the word *shake* was synonymous with getting a treat. Whenever he'd hear me say this word, he'd quickly put up his paw.

Next, while he was standing I'd give Kernel the command to sit. At first he didn't know what that meant. So I gently pushed his hind legs into a sitting position. That was always rewarded with a treat. It was the easiest of all the tricks, and it took him only two days to learn it.

Getting him to sit up was a little more difficult, because he had a tendency to fall sideways. So I had to hold him in that position for a few seconds. Then I would tell him to stay. This was the most difficult trick for him to learn.

Teaching Kernel to roll over took longer. First I managed to get him to lie down, and then I'd roll him over. After doing that for about a week, he would still lie there but not roll on his own. It took another week of me turning him before he finally started to roll over.

I also taught Kernel to respond to hand signals. I'd tell him to stay, and then I'd walk a few steps and call him. No problem— when I called him, he'd come running. Then I would move farther away and make a motion with my hand. At first I both used a signal and called. Soon I could just the hand signal.

Of course, a boy could also learn a lot from a wolf:

Loyalty, obedience, patience.

Turn around three times around before you lie down.

Take a bath, and then go roll around in something rotten!

———

By the summer of 1935, Kernel was about two and a half years old. His coat was darker now, and he weighed close to seventy-five pounds. The gunshot wound he had sustained was completely healed, but he would have to be taught to fear cars and other people. Each time I heard a car approaching, I'd run and hide, then point to the car and shout, "Bad car!" This routine went on all summer. One day he "woofed" at me for no reason, or so I thought. Then I heard a car approaching, and he ran for the bushes before the car was in sight. Now that's what I call good training. Or maybe it was just smart thinking by a wolf.

Some people tell me a dog's worst enemy is his master. I half-way agree with them. I was determined to be a good master for my wolf. I had to be protective, or at least careful. One day we encountered a skunk. This is the only fearless animal in the world, and we were about to find out why. We tried to avoid a confrontation, but the skunk let out a squirt in our direction. Kernel sensed it was going to attack me, and as usual he came to my rescue. Before I could stop him, he tried to attack it. He soon paid the price. He started to cough, and so did I. It was so hard to breathe, I had to rush over to the river and throw Kernel in.

When we got home, my mother knew what had happened before we entered the house. She made me change clothes and gave me a fly sprayer that contained some kind of mixture. Whatever it was, it helped stop the odor.

A porcupine is said to be an Indian's best friend. Yet it can be a dog's worst enemy. On our way to our fishing hole, Kernel ran ahead and met up with a porcupine. He came back to me with a muzzle full of quills. He tried to rub them off on the ground. I ran home and got a pair of pliers to pull them out. While I did this, he just stood and let me pull them out of him. He seemed to understand that I was helping him. Each time I pulled one out it made him bleed, so I'd put a cold, wet cloth on it until the bleeding stopped. He never whimpered and seemed to know what had to be done. I was thankful he didn't have any in his eyes.

One day at the frog pond, I was startled by a big pine snake. It could have been the same one that had scared my sister a year earlier. Kernel noticed when I jumped, and he came running over and saw the snake near my foot. He circled it and got it by the side of its head and threw it in the air. He did this several times, and then I noticed foam coming from his mouth. I thought he had rabies, so I ran home and told my mother what happened. She just laughed and replied, "Don't worry! That's just his way of protecting himself from poison."

Another day, while I was sitting by the river watching some birds building a nest, I noticed a car approaching and looked to see if Kernel was anywhere nearby. He was hiding. A white man got out and asked if he could have a picnic at the spot where I was sitting. I got up and said, "It's all yours." Then I added, "You don't mind sharing it with a wolf, do you?"

"A wolf?" he shouted. He turned to see Kernel standing there, sniffing the air. Now, this was a big white man, and when he saw Kernel, he turned even whiter. He hurried back to his car. I knew he was scared, and I tried to assure him that Kernel would not harm anyone. He didn't seem convinced, so I told Kernel to sit. Then I told him to roll over. The white man still wasn't convinced. I told him that Kernel just wanted to shake his hand. "Really?" he asked. I warned him to give Kernel a tidbit to reward him. He reached into the backseat and got a piece of a sandwich. After he shook hands with Kernel, he told me, "No one will ever believe I shook hands with a real wolf!"

With a fishing pole on my shoulder and my wolf at my side, who could ask for anything more? We were two lone wolves and didn't give a hoot about anything—well, except skunks and porcupines. We fished and hunted a lot the rest of that summer. Sometimes we would just sit and watch the clouds roll by. When I looked at the sky, Kernel would sit by my side and look in the direction of my gaze and to see if there were any partridges.

These memorable times are etched in my mind, and I'll always cherish them. Sometimes I reminisce, picturing my wolf sitting in the snow or sitting by the river or just jumping around in our back yard. There will never be another one like him.

24

Model A

The year 1936 was like any other, until my brother-in-law, Melvin, bought another Model A, a 1931 Tudor. Mel made frequent trips to and from Wittenberg, about thirty miles from my home, and on one of these trips he asked me to drive. Remembering what he taught me on the 1929 Model A, I got behind the wheel. This old four-cylinder had a stick shift on the floor. Now that I could reach the pedals a little easier, it made a world of difference in shifting. Melvin put his jacket behind me, which helped me turn the steering wheel better. Then he said, "Let's go!"

"The shift pattern is in an 'H' form, right?" I asked.

"Right. One, two, three, and reverse is up to the left."

He let me drive the rest of the way to his home in Wittenberg, and then back to my home. I pulled up to our house, and my mother gasped when she noticed I was driving.

"We have a new driver," Mel told my mother. "All he needs is a little more practice."

Next I had to get a driver's permit. I had to study the road and hand signals and the little handbook on the rules and signs of the road. The most important thing was not to pass on hills, curves, railroad tracks, or in intersections.

You didn't need a driver's license to drive on the reservation, but I wanted one. "Next time you go to Shawano, take me along so I can take this test," I told Mel. He said we'd go the next day. I had a hard time getting to sleep that night.

The next morning, Mel said, "Shawano County Courthouse, here we come!" On the way there, Mel asked me to identify all the road signs. The most important one, he told me, was the stop sign. "Look," he said, "it has eight sides. The round one is a railroad sign, it has an 'X' on it that means crossing." Mel dropped me off at the sheriff's office and advised, "You're on your own. They might keep me in there."

As I approached the main desk, I asked, "Where do I take the driver's test?" The woman receptionist answered, "For whom?" I told her it would be for me. "Aren't you a little young to be driving?" she scolded. With a look of great determination, I boldly claimed, "I'll be fourteen next year."

The sheriff walked in, and the woman told him "this little boy" would like to take the driver's test. He looked at me and told me to follow him. We sat down at a table, and he opened up a book and asked, "What's the stop sign look like?"

"It's red and has eight sides with 'STOP' written on it."

"Not bad. What's a railroad sign look like?"

"It's round and white with a cross on it."

He looked impressed. "What's an intersection?"

"That's when two lines cross. They form 90-degree angles."

"What are you, some kind of wise guy?" he asked.

I told him, "I never smart off to police officers."

"Okay. When does the law permit you to drive on the left side?"

"When you pass, when the road is under construction, or when a policeman directs you to."

"When are you not supposed to pass another car?"

"On a hill, curve, railroad, or intersection."

He smiled. "You just passed your driver's test."

"When can I start driving?"

"Here's a note that will serve as your driver's license. Your permit will be mailed to you within a week."

With that note in my hand, I rushed out of the courthouse and ran down the steps and tripped over the last step and fell into a rosebush. When I got up, a cop was standing there. He asked me if I had been drinking. I dusted myself off and said, "I just passed my driver's test." Looking bewildered, he advised me to not drive for a while.

Now to find Mel and tell him the good news. Let's see. There were only two taverns in Shawano that he frequented. I hit the first bar, and there he sat with a glass of beer in his hand. With the note held high, I bragged, "Look, I just passed my driver's test!" He took it from my hand to read it and was about to hand it back to me when the bartender asked if he could see it. Mel handed it to him, and he said, "Well, I'll be."

When my driver's permit arrived, it looked like a regular license, except it was printed in red. This permit could be used only during daylight hours. In order to drive at night, I had to have an older person with me. My brothers never had driver's licenses because they didn't need one while driving on the reservation. That might explain why they got into so many wrecks!

For me this was the beginning of a newfound pleasure and

also a profitable sideline transporting lumberjacks to and from the logging camps. But my good news made my mother worried. She thought I was too young to drive. She changed her mind once we needed transportation and no one else could drive outside the reservation.

When she was convinced I could handle a car, she said, "Maybe we can buy you one." But how would we pay for it? We saved all summer to buy a car. This included part of my cherry-picking money and some of my beadwork funds. People hired me to drive them to and from the nearby cities. Soon I had managed to save enough for a car, even though I had never even owned a bicycle.

Not long after cherry-picking time was over, my mother told me to ask Melvin to take us to Shawano.

"We'll be looking at cars," she said.

25

Ray's Taxi

After searching a while for a suitable car, we found a light blue 1932 Chevrolet coupe with spare tires on each front fender and a luggage rack behind the rumble seat. It was love at first sight and began my never-ending love affair with cars. Who needs women when you have a car like this? Whenever I polished or washed my car, my mother would say, "You're not working on that car, you're romancing it!" She was right. I even slept in it the first night.

My mother put down a thirty-five-dollar deposit. The balance was forty dollars, and we had to make monthly payments of ten dollars. The logging camps were located about four to ten miles from Neopit, and the lumberjacks were paid on the first and fifteenth of each month. They needed someone to pick them up and take them to the nearby towns. This was where I came in. I made two payments in one week. Now all I owed was twenty dollars.

Lots of those old boys at the logging camps were robbed after they passed out, so they welcomed a young man like me who didn't drink and who would look out for them while they were drinking. One day I met the sheriff near a tavern, and he asked how my driving was coming along. I told him that I was taking care of some lumberjacks. He told me to be careful and watch out when they got drunk. "Don't let them steal your car!" he warned me.

Many people hired me to take them to the city to buy provisions. The Chevy got a workout, and people paid me a dollar for a round trip. Gas was ten cents a gallon. I was doing pretty well with Ray's Taxi.

———

The famous White House, of course, is where the president lives and where all our problems are supposed to be resolved. Men enter the White House with predicaments and leave with frowns on their faces.

But the White House I'm talking about housed some of the most attractive "ladies of the night" in our area. This house of pleasure was located near the city of Antigo, not too far from the reservation. And at this White House, men entered with an expression of anxiety and left with smiles that would take an undertaker three days to wipe off.

The ladies of the night were meticulous about their appearance and what little attire they wore. Even their manners were admirable. These women showed their appreciation for my presence each time my old Chevy brought them a carload of lumberjacks. They would give me a candy bar, comic books, and soda. Most of them knew my name. Some even asked about my schoolwork.

The madam, mistress of the brothel, displayed a fond affection for me each time I had the pleasure of meeting her. She smelled of perfume that made me gasp for air. She had such benevolent regard for me that one day she handed me a present wrapped in a box with a bow on it. "Merry Christmas, Ray," she said, and I smiled and thanked her. She never told me her name, so I just referred to her as "Ma'am."

The madam could be ferocious when provoked, as I soon found out. (When things go too smoothly—beware! My mother's old adage proved accurate again.) One night we heard a roar of engines outside and looked out to see about five squad cars. The door burst open and one agent hollered, "This is a raid!"

The first agent in the door tried to grab the madam, and she belted him so hard he flew clear out the door, only to be replaced by another. It took four agents to subdue her. Before they placed her in the squad car, one of the agents grabbed me by my arm and said, "Look, I got a kid!"

"Let go of him, you son of a bitch!" the madam cried, and then she hit him so hard he bounced off the wall.

"How many men do you got in here?" the sheriff asked me. "Four," I answered.

The sheriff said, "Take them all to the jail and wait for me there."

As I left, I could see some of the men pulling up their longjohns as they were pushed into waiting squad cars. As I passed the squad car where the madam was, she was still swinging at the agents. They probably wouldn't have had a workout like that if they'd cornered a black bear. To make matters worse, they were going to have a hell of a time explaining why they reeked of her perfume.

I managed to get all four of my passengers out of jail before the night was over. They all paid their fines for disorderly conduct—a dollar each, or about one day's pay.

Two days later, the White House was once again open for business.

I know because I took another bunch of lumberjacks there.

———

The Green Roof, in Shawano County, was another house of ill fame. Everyone seemed to know about it. The lumberjacks had their choice of the White House or the Green Roof, and most preferred the latter. It was my job to get them there and back and look out for "poachers"—men who prey on other men for their money.

One day at the crack of noon, I was parked near the pay station waiting for my first passenger, and I spotted a poacher. He was easy to recognize, because he didn't have work clothes on. My first two customers sat in the front seat, and I asked them if they knew the guy. Both answered no. "We'd better keep an eye on him," I said, and they agreed. He approached my car and asked if I had room for another. I told him, sure, but he had to pay first. He reached into his pocket and said, "All I have is a twenty."

I knew he didn't have a twenty, so I told him to give me the twenty and I'd change it for him. He told me he'd be right back. We all laughed as he walked away.

But to my surprise, he came back a few minutes later and handed me fifty cents. He got in the rumble seat. All I had to do was wait for one more customer. That didn't take long, and soon we were on our way to the first tavern. Before we went in, I told the two men to watch and see if that guy had any money. Turned out I was right. He didn't have enough to buy a beer. We dumped him right there.

The Green Roof did not have a madam or mistress. It was operated by a man, and he was one mean S.O.B. I know because I watched as he bounced many men out the door. He stood six feet tall and weighed about two hundred pounds. The first time I met him he told me, "You can't come in here, boy!"

I looked him straight in the eye and said, "Then from now on I'll take all my passengers to the White House instead."

He backed off. "You mean to tell me that you brought me some customers?"

"All four of 'em!" I snapped.

He scratched his head and said, "Well, I'll be a son of a bitch." He pointed toward the bar and told me to go in. "Tell the bartender to give you anything you want." Once I was in the bar, the bartender looked at me and told me that he couldn't serve me. Just then the Big Man himself walked in and asked me why I hadn't gotten myself a Coke. I told him that the bartender wouldn't serve me. "What?" he shouted, turning to the bartender. "Give him anything he wants, and don't charge him!" Meekly, the bartender served me a Coke and some potato chips.

After the men came down from upstairs, we headed for the door. As we were about to depart, the Big Man hollered "Ray!" I ran back to see what he wanted. He bent down and took out a big roll of bills, peeled off one, and handed it to me. "Thanks," I said with a smile on my face. "I'll bring you another load this weekend."

The Big Man smiled back. "You do that, and I'll make it right with you."

26

Saturday Night

My little Chevy was the talk of my peers. They all wanted to ride in it, and they also wanted to see my driver's permit. I didn't disappoint them. Now we could go to the lakes or to the nearest city for a movie. What more could a quiet little Indian boy ask for?

A Saturday night dance in Gresham, that's what. Get some of the boys together and see what we could come up with. We would need a siphon hose to drain someone's gas tank while they were dancing up a storm. (*Good thinking, Ray!*) But first we would need enough gas to get there. Oh, well, it was only ten cents a gallon.

John Smash was always good for a couple dimes. Big Chevy (Harvey) could be counted on for another dime or two. When we got to the dancehall, all we had to do was wait until dark, position a lookout, and start siphoning gas. The Model As were the easy ones because they had tanks on the hood, behind and above the engine. We always displayed etiquette, never draining a tank completely. Leave enough for the man to get home.

With a tank full of gas, we could go and fraternize with the "palefaces" and maybe even dance a couple of songs and hope it didn't rain. (An Indian has to be careful, you know.)

What's a Saturday night without a good fight? On this night the polka band was whooping it up, and all the people were in the mood for action. One guy swung his girlfriend around and forgot to hold onto her. She fell on her ass, got up, and took another guy for a partner like nothing happened. Two girls were whirling around and around until they got dizzy and wound up under a table. Some old gal was dancing up a storm, and her stockings fell down to her ankles. Some girl even lost her panties. I know because I tripped on them.

Back in the thirties, the dancehalls didn't have air conditioning. On this hot summer night, everyone was starting to sweat, and no one had deodorant. Let me tell you this: the lumberjacks worked all week without taking a bath or shower, and they smelled better than a lot of those old gals at the dance. Also, the drunker they got, the more daring they got. One guy kept whirling his girlfriend right off her feet. This happened once too often, for soon he lost his balance and threw her right into the bandstand. She hit the drummer and knocked down the trumpet player.

Then the real fun began. Smash goosed a gal, and she turned and belted a guy behind her. He hit her partner, and then two other guys joined in the fight. Soon the whole dance floor was swinging, and it wasn't to the tune of the music. Smash headed for the door, followed by Harvey, and I started in the same direction. "Grab a few bottles on the way out!" Harvey yelled, and I added, "Don't forget the Coke!"

Now what? We had enough gas to go to another dancehall, so we headed for the one on Highway 29 just east of Shawano. This place was a little more expensive. The lady at the front held her hand out and said, "It will cost you five cents." I pointed to the dance floor and told her, "I'll have to get it from my mother. She's in the hall." She gave me permission, and I went in.

Harvey and Smash sneaked in, too, and we met on the side of the dance floor, just in time to hear the bandleader announce that the next dance would be Ladies' Choice. Everyone had a partner except for one fat lady who was standing close to me. She had sweat pouring off her forehead, and her armpits were soaked. She jerked me toward her, and I wound up with my nose between her large, sweaty breasts. As she whirled me around like a ragdoll, I saw Smash and Harvey pointing at me and laughing their asses off. What a humiliating situation! Bet my wolf wouldn't have anything to do with me once I got home. My feet touched the floor maybe once or twice during the whole dance.

We figured we had better check on the car before someone drained *our* tank, so we headed outside. There we caught two guys with their hose still stuck in my tank. I asked one of them how much gas he took. "None," he said. Harvey grabbed the hose and gas can, threw them on the rumble seat, and said, "Now they won't be draining any more tanks." Then he declared that he and Smash needed a few more beers. So Smash headed back to the dance and came back with a case. I opened the rumble seat, and he dropped it in. "Where's my Coke?" I asked. He muttered an obscenity and went back to get me three bottles.

Now all I had to do was dodge the drunk drivers on the way back home, a maneuver that felt like driving the wrong way on the expressway during rush hour. Finally I dropped off Smash and Harvey. They poured out of the car, waved, and said, "See ya tomorrow!"

When I got home, my mother was still awake. She asked me where I had been.

"Working," I told her. "And I got a full tank of gas."

My wolf sniffed me and sneezed.

"You don't smell so good," my mother remarked.

"I know," I sighed, "I tangled with a hog."

She gave me a mean look. "Better stay away from those pigpens!"

I was already wondering what was going to happen the next Saturday night when my mother said, "You'd better think about going to back to school."

At least there was one good thing about returning to school. This time I wouldn't have to walk.

27

High School Years

When the fall semester of 1936 began, I started seventh grade at the high school in Keshena.* I will always remember my first day there, thanks to the compassionate help of a girl named Clarabelle. The teacher ordered me to the blackboard. With a piece of chalk in my hand, I stood there waiting. Then the teacher said, "Raymond, write out an algebraic expression!" To this day, I can still feel the tension I felt as I stood before the class, not knowing anything about algebra. But Clarabelle was sitting close by, and she whispered some letters and numbers. I wrote them on the board. They were all correct.

Clarabelle was not only intelligent but was the most attractive girl in our class. She was also the most affluent. She drove a brand new black two-door Ford and even gave me a ride in it one day. I admired her throughout high school and still do to this day.

Throughout my younger years I regarded girls as frail people who could get hurt easily. They seemed so dainty to me, and all of them reminded me of my little sister. So I treated them all with respect and remained aloof. Then I met a girl named Delores. She

---

* St. Joseph's Indian Industrial School at Keshena was a Catholic mission school established in 1883.

was tiny, and so was I. We were the smallest in our class, and this gave us something in common. Her face would put any movie star's to shame. Delores was always polite and would dance with me at the school dances. We even shared a Coke or two.

Another head-turner in my class was Roberta. Her grandparents had a home across the highway from ours. Roberta spent the summers with them, and we shared many happy hours swimming in the Wolf River. Roberta's grandfather had great respect for my driving ability. Many times I drove him to Shawano and Antigo. On one of those trips we encountered two ladies of the night from the Green Roof. Both of them said, "Hi, Ray," and I said hello back. Grandpa Waukau exclaimed, "They look like whores!"

"They are," I explained. "They work at the Green Roof."

"How do you know?"

"Because I take all the lumberjacks there."

He smiled and said, "For a while there, I was beginning to wonder about you."

———

One of my teachers had told me not to park on the school grounds, so I always parked about a block from school. One day when I looked for my car, it was missing. I had to walk home. I told my mother someone had stolen my car, and she said. "Your brother must have taken it." I told her it had almost a full tank of gas. "That's why he took it," she added. This disgusted me, planting seeds of hatred toward my brothers. They never had driver's licenses, and every time they drove they'd get drunk and wreck the car. I wondered how bad my car was going to get wrecked this time.

Early the next morning, I heard a car pull up to the front of the house. I quickly went to survey the damage. I noticed that a front tire was flat, and the wheel was completely ruined. The ignition was torn up, and my radiator ornament was missing. So was the gas! It was a pathetic sight, and it made me sick and angry. When my mother saw the condition my car was in, she said, "I'll have a talk with him." I thought that was like giving a dog a bone for peeing on the carpet.

When I asked my brother why he hadn't changed the tire, he told me, "I didn't feel like it." My anger grew.

"You feel like helping me change it now?" I asked.

He gave me a stern look and snapped, "It's your car. You change it!"

With one flat tire and the ignition torn out, I decided to leave the Chevy parked until spring. I drained the radiator and the block and took out the battery. If my brother was too lazy to change a tire, he'd never have the motivation to fix the rest of the car, so I knew the Chevy would be safe.

He often asked me why I didn't just change the tire. I'd tell him, "I don't feel like it." This would get him annoyed. He just couldn't wait to wreck it, and I wasn't sure why. Then I realized that he must have been jealous. He had never owned a car.

———

Since the Keshena school was operated by the Catholic Church, Christmas was one of the highlights of the year. Naturally, we had to adhere to their religious methods, attending Mass, saying prayers before classes, and taking religious studies. The Mother Superior would have been proud of me. I never did learn when to correctly stand, sit, or kneel, though. I hope she'd forgive me for that.

About this time, my mother told me she was thinking about buying another car. She had just enough to put a down payment on a 1931 Ford Model A coupe with a rumble seat. It wasn't as good as a Chevy, but good enough. I was soon back in the taxi business. I made two dollars during the first trip and the same amount for the second. The madam at the White House was glad to see me again. Even some of the other ladies said, "Hi, Ray!" The Big Man at the Green Roof also remembered me and gave me a dollar each time I delivered four lumberjacks to his establishment.

One day I took my mother out to do some shopping in Antigo, and we encountered a couple ladies of the night. They both smiled and greeted me. After they passed by, my mother scolded, "Those women are whores." I smiled and said, "I know." My mother asked me where I met them. "At the White House, where I take all the lumberjacks," I explained. "That's how I make two dollars a trip." My mother wasn't very happy but seemed relieved.

The Model A got a workout during the fall and well into the next year. By that time I had earned enough money to have it all paid for, but with two brothers at home who drank heavily and with no one to control them, how could we cope? We couldn't. They did as they pleased.

Starting in fall 1937 I attended school at Neopit. One day while I was at school, my brothers took the car to Shawano. They bought some wine and got so liquored up that they totaled the car. I was forced to walk to school again. Now what was I going to do? I started saving up for another one. This time I was determined that my brothers were not to borrow it under any circumstance.

Then, just before Thanksgiving 1938, we had a stroke of good luck. Melvin wanted to buy another car and sell his old one. I needed a car to get back in business, so we bought it. I had that car until the spring of 1941. I thought it would make it until that summer, but one day I returned from school to find it missing, along with my brothers. At the end of May they still had not returned. We knew they had to be in jail, so Melvin drove me there. Both my brothers had been sent to jail for charges of public drunkenness, driving without a license, property damage, and resisting arrest. They needed bail money, so I told them I would work hard that summer to help bail them out.

Instead, I used the money I saved to get the Model A fixed and drove it until they got out. When they were released in September, they asked me why I hadn't bailed them out like I had promised. "I had to get the car fixed so I could make the money," I told them. This didn't please them one bit, and I knew that they were planning on wrecking the car again.

In September 1941 my eldest sister left home and went to the convent. With a heart full of sadness, I called for my wolf and walked to the riverbank. I sat there for a long time, thinking that maybe Mary, too, was fed up with all the drinking. I felt like crying and fought back my tears. Only girls cry. I thought my wolf understood my feelings.

28

Aviary Clan

By that fall of 1941 I had become more like a man and had lost my angelic voice. It was time for me to find out who I was. This was the time in my life when the boy in me died and the man in me came alive.

What I'm about to relate was practiced by my family and wasn't considered traditional by many other Menominee Indians. Remember, my mother was a Medicine Woman who made most of her own rules. We held the annual Medicine Lodge, where no women were permitted to enter. The lodge was like a steam bath. It was there that we would fast and meditate.

Early one morning, after I started speaking with a deeper voice, my mother said, "Raymond, you are about to find out what you are." I told her that I already knew what I was and that I didn't need to know anything more. "Listen to me," she said sternly. "As of now, you are not to come into this house or eat or drink anything until you have a vision. Once you start, your first vision will be of food; your next vision will shed light on what you are. Do you under-stand?" I nodded my head, and, taking only the clothes I had on me, I left.

She was right. The first night I did dream of food. The next day I roamed the riverbanks and took long hikes to Camp 4 Hill.

Hoping to prevent any disturbance of my forthcoming vision, I stayed out of view of everyone. The second night, the insects kept me awake, but by morning I dreamed of a large bird. As I looked up into the clear blue sky, I noticed a hawk circling above me. It didn't move its wings much, just soared around for a long time. Then it started to dive, and just before it got to the ground, it spread its wings, stretching its feet out, and picked up a mouse.

This was the vision I was looking for. That's when I knew what I was. Some people belong to the Wolf clan, some the Bear clan, others the Eagle clan. I knew I must be of the Aviary (Bird) clan—the Hawk.

When I got home, I told my mother the good news about my vision.

"You are from the Hawk family. You are now called Little Hawk," she said.

With all this excitement, I forgot about my hunger for a while, but then I went into the kitchen. "Today you eat alone," my mother said. "Tomorrow you will feel like a new man. That is, if you don't already." I didn't know if I would feel like a new man. All I knew was hunger, and right about then even a mouse was looking good to me. But she was right. I did feel like I had achieved something. At least I had a new name.

Even my little sister remarked, "You look different."

"That's because I'm hungry. I've been out for two nights without any food, and all I had to drink was river water," I informed her.

I noticed my wolf was waiting for me on the steps of the back porch. He wagged his tail as I approached, seeming to say, *Welcome back.* I sat beside him, and he hit me with his paw. I put my arm around him and said, "We must never kill a hawk." His tail swooshed as if he understood.

"You talking to that old wolf again?" my little sister asked. "Don't you know he can't understand you?" I told her he understood everything I said to him. She shook her head and walked away, saying, "You're both crazy."

"No!" I shouted back, "I'm Little Hawk!" Pointing at the sky, I added, "Someday I will fly like the hawk around those clouds." She just shook her head again as if she couldn't understand.

29

Baraboo

My seventeenth birthday had just passed, and already I was looking forward to my eighteenth so I could leave home and get a job far away from my brothers. Cherry-picking time was over, and we had enough money to get the car fixed. For a while I drove to school, but I knew it was just a matter of time before one of my brothers would wreck the car. There was no way I could stop them, and they knew it. My anger at them had grown. Somehow my car stayed in good shape until December 7, 1941. That was the day the Japanese did a good job of bombing Pearl Harbor. That was also the day my brother did a good job on my car. He got bombed and drove it into a ditch.

That's it. I've had it. I can't take it anymore! I told myself. When I announced to my mother that I was leaving home, she convinced me to stay until the end of the semester. Reluctantly, I agreed.

In January I heard of a place called Baraboo in south-central Wisconsin. Someone told me people were being hired to work in a defense plant where they made powder and rockets for the war. In spring 1942 I decided to hitchhike there and apply for a job. So I said good-bye to my wolf and left.

It was the first time I had left my wolf alone. I wondered how he would react to my absence. I wrote a letter home to my mother. She later told me that when Kernel smelled the letter, he knew it was from me.

When I applied for a job at the Badger Ordnance Works, they told me that because I was underage I needed a work permit. The courthouse in Baraboo issued me a form to be signed by my mother. I stopped at a restaurant and had a cup of coffee, signed the form, and took it back to the courthouse. They looked it over and issued me the work permit.

With the permit in my hand, I headed for the Badger Ordnance Works and was immediately hired. The pay was seventy-five cents an hour, with payday every Thursday. The plant was still under construction, and that was where I worked, building reinforcements around each storehouse of ammunition. My first paycheck was forty-two dollars after deductions, and the Social Security tax was a penny for each dollar I made. I felt like a millionaire. This was more money than the lumberjacks made all month! After my rent was paid, all I had to do was head for the movie theater downtown or shop around for some new clothes. Still, on my first payday I thought of my little sister and my mother. I got a money order of ten dollars and sent it out to them in the evening mail. Now I didn't have much left.

After a few weeks of collecting my huge profits, I had money in a checking account and money in my pocket, but I lacked something else—a girlfriend. After watching the women walk by in their silk stockings with the black seams up the back, I decided to go out hunting for one.

Let's see. There was one I saw often at a restaurant. Her name was Alice. But how do you go about asking a girl out for the evening? Easy, just go over and start talking to her. First, call her by her name: "Alice . . ."

"Yes, Ray, what can I do for you?"

"I . . . I . . ."

"Would you like a date with me?"

"How'd you know that?"

"I was hoping you'd ask someday."

"How about Saturday night?"

"Fine. I'd like to go to the Al Ringling Theatre."

"See you Saturday night, about seven!"

The next day at work, I started drilling a hole in the concrete we had put in the week before. The foreman asked where my brains were. "I guess I was thinking about Saturday night," I told him.

"Oh, yeah? What's so special about Saturday night?" he asked.

With a big smile on my face, I told him I had a date with the most beautiful girl in town. He huffed, "That explains it. Better not use the jackhammer today—you might blow up the whole plant!"

When Saturday arrived, I was a little nervous for the date. As I prepared, I grabbed a tube of hair cream and commenced to brush my teeth. It tasted bitter and didn't get my teeth too clean. When I arrived at the restaurant, I sat at the counter, and the guy next to me said, "Are you advertising, or do you always walk around with your fly open?"

Alice arrived, and we walked to the Al Ringling Theatre to see *Trail of the Lonesome Pine,* starring John Wayne and Betty Field. The movie was kind of sad and made Alice shed a tear or two. After the movie, we strolled over to a tavern just off Baraboo's downtown square. I was only seventeen but had a badge from work with my picture on it. They thought I was old enough, and who cared, really? It was wartime.

If I'm with a woman, some guy will always try to pick her up. As we drank our beers, a guy walked over and asked Alice who the dumb Indian was sitting next to her.

"His name is Ray, and he's a lot smarter than you," she answered.

"Well, I don't like smart guys," he grumbled.

Like I always say, I can be minding my own business, and some guy will hit me from behind when I'm not expecting it. The man knocked me off balance, and I wound up on the floor. Alice rushed to pick me up, and I asked her who hit me. She pointed to the guy. That was all I needed to know. "You're not going to let him get away with that, are you?" Alice asked.

"Alice," I said, "calm down. Church isn't over 'til they quit singing." I told her to move closer to the guy.

"So, you're the dumb Indian," he said to me.

"No, I just came to ask you for the next dance."

"What?"

"Well, Alice here said you wanted to dance with me."

He called Alice a derogatory name. Unfortunately for him, Alice heard it and knocked him ass over teakettle. (Alice had brothers who were boxers, and she knew how to make a fist and deliver it.) Now the man was on the floor, looking up at the chandelier. I asked Alice why she socked him. "Because he wouldn't dance with you," she answered. I told her once he got back up, I'd ask him again, except this time politely. The man's lip was bleeding, and he staggered back to the bar. He was about to sit down when I asked, "Now, before Alice knocks you down again, will you dance with me?"

That got him going! "Why, you son of a . . . ," he muttered as he drew his arm back. Before he could get close to delivering his punch, I clipped him with a left hook to the jaw. He wound up back on the floor.

The bartender came over and asked, "Who started this fight?" Alice pointed to the guy on the floor and said, "He did! He won't dance with Ray." The bartender looked puzzled and walked back behind the bar. Alice was grinning.

"Alice," I turned to her, "that guy just doesn't like to dance."

"Maybe he thinks you want to lead."

"Yeah. Wait'll he gets up. I'll show him how to do the Menominee waltz!"

She laughed, "I love the way you put that."

The next day I looked in the mirror and, to my surprise, I didn't have a black eye. Then I tried to pick up a cup of coffee only to find that my fingers were too sore to lift it. Still, not too bad for a Saturday night. I thought about how my wolf had to fight when he had no other alternative. He never provoked a fight, and I'm the same. That's another thing you can learn from a wolf.

During that spring I dated other girls, but Alice was the most outstanding. One night I got in a fight with another woman's ex-boyfriend. The woman told me she didn't want to see me anymore. With a bleeding lip, I headed toward the door, and there stood Alice. She gave me a disgusted look and asked, "Having a nice time?"

"No, that guy didn't want to dance."

"You're still bleeding," she said, teasing me.

I tried to smile. "Not as bad as him."

"You need someone to look after you," Alice said. She handed me her handkerchief, and we headed out the door and got a cab. I told her proudly that I was a lone wolf and didn't need anyone. "But you certainly look like you do," she said. I told her that the guy hit me when I wasn't looking. "Just like the last time," she said, putting her arm around my neck. "See what trouble you get in when I'm not around?" She smiled. "Try calling me once in a while."

We dated the rest of the summer and into the fall.

As we sat on a park bench with the leaves falling all around us, Alice took my hand and said, "Ray, I'd like to be someone's wife." I knew then that she was serious, so I put my arm around her shoulder and gave her a little squeeze. Then I told her something—something I had done that would change my life.

"Alice," I said, "when I turned seventeen, I decided to go to war."

"So you enlisted?"

"Yes."

"What branch of service?"

"The Marines."

Alice did not seem pleased. "Of all the branches of service, you had to pick the toughest!"

"Well, Indians fight a lot," I told her.

I had gone to enlist that summer, just before my birthday, but the Marine Corps said I needed my mother's consent, so I went back when I turned eighteen. Then the Marines had to find out if I had a criminal background, which took about a month and a half. Finally they requested that I make an appearance at an office in Milwaukee. They told me to bring my birth certificate and to be prepared to take a complete physical examination.

Anticipating the big day made me as nervous as a June bride. At five feet, eight inches tall, I wasn't sure they would take me, but all the doctors who examined me gave me their approval. One asked me, "You sure you want to go into the Marines?" I smiled eagerly and nodded. I passed the physical exam and was sent back home to await further orders.

30

Boot Camp

By late 1942, Barney Ross was making headlines in the local and national newspapers. The boxing champion from Chicago was in the Marines and had already seen action on Guadalcanal.

Finally, in March 1943, I received orders to report to the Federal Building in Milwaukee. Outside the Federal Building were a bunch of draftees. A man standing there with a clipboard hollered: "Get back in line!" I asked what for. He looked at me and asked me if I was from the reservation. I told him I was and that I was there to enlist in the Marines. That didn't go over well. "You're going into the Army whether you like it or not," he said. Then a policeman walked up and asked what was going on.

"This man here is trying to dodge the draft," the man with the clipboard accused.

"Are you with these draftees?" asked the policeman.

"No, I'm here to enlist in the Marines," I answered.

"Mister, do you have papers on this man?" the policeman asked the man with the clipboard.

"No, but he's from the reservation, and I have charge of him."

"Not unless you have his draft papers."

"Sir," I piped up, "I signed up for the Marines, and here are my papers."

"Go join the Marines!" said the policeman.

The man with the clipboard didn't like that one bit. "I'll get you for this," he promised.

Once inside the building, I didn't know where to go. The place was so big I got lost right from the start. There were so many rooms that I couldn't locate the one for the Marines. Someone told me to stand in line for a physical. Just then a Marine sergeant came along, and I told him I had already had a physical. He looked at my papers and agreed. "All you need is swearing in," he said, motioning for me to follow him.

A tall man standing in line with me remarked, "The Marines want men like me."

"He's about to become a Marine," the sergeant told him. The tall man didn't have anything more to say about that.

After being cleared by the Marine recruiters, a group of us were sent to the Juneau Hotel on East Wisconsin Avenue. The next day, we had breakfast and then boarded the train for San Diego. We had our own sleeping bunks and meal tickets. Who could ask for anything more? On the way to California, we took the northern route, which took us through a mountain pass drifted and blocked with snow. The engineer had to wait to get help from two snowplows, but we made it through. This trip was the most exciting and longest sojourn of my teenage life, but I was not alone. Most of the other men were also in their teens. The oldest was twenty.

Our trip across the country took about four days and nights. As we peered out the windows toward the mountains, rivers, lakes, and forests, the changing scenes seemed endless. At times I thought about my wolf, and I hoped he'd understand why I had to leave. I knew he'd be there when I got back.

One day someone said, "Look! That's Salt Lake." I knew we must be in Salt Lake City. It didn't look all that different from Lake Michigan. When we saw oranges in the trees, we knew we were finally in California. What a place! The warm breeze made it feel like it was the middle of summer. When we got off the train, green trucks were waiting to take us to a Marine Corps base near the Pacific Ocean, located near an airplane factory that produced B-24 bombers.

Our tent area was next to the runways. The B-24 had four engines, and each engine had about 3,500 horsepower. Multiply that by four and you can imagine how loud they sounded on takeoff. As the planes cleared the ground, we could see the pilots, and sometimes we could see them wave at us. When one of the bombers was ready for shipment, it was sent out, day or night. This meant the loud takeoffs happened a lot, and at times we had trouble sleeping. One day I heard tires squealing and saw a bomber getting so close to the fence it almost hit it. The takeoff was aborted due to the plane being overweight.

Walking toward our new lodging, some boots (trainees) hollered, "You'll be sorry!" A guy next to me said, "Ray, now is the time for all good men to get the hell out of here." But so far, I had no complaints. The weather was perfect, the food delicious, and we were all issued new clothes. Soon would come the bad part, though: the inoculations.

While waiting in line, a tall man standing in front of me fell over. I tried to catch him when he fell, but I was too late, and he crashed to the floor. Someone else started to vomit, and just watching him made me feel sick. After receiving all of my shots and a blood test, I knew what it felt like to be a pincushion. We all walked back to the huts holding a piece of cotton on our arms.

We were issued two oval-shaped brass tags. On each one was printed our last name with first and middle initials, blood type, religion ("C" for Catholic, "P" for Protestant), serial number, and branch of service. Mine said USMC.

We also had to have our hair cut. It was like getting scalped by a white man. But I lucked out. My barber was from Wisconsin, and after he found out I was from Baraboo, he just gave me a nice crew cut.

The day after I got my shots, I started to run a fever and felt nauseous and very weak. My temperature was 104, and I was taken to the sick bay. One day a nun took a blood sample, and she reminded me of the nuns at the Keshena Hospital. I wondered if the Mother Superior had trained her.

I lost about ten pounds while I was in the infirmary. Although I felt weak, after ten days I was discharged and sent back to my platoon. The doctors recommended light duty for one week, and this meant I didn't have to do any long marches, calisthenics, running, and no fighting of any kind. All the guys teased me about being a Sick Bay Marine.

Two days after I was put on light duty, someone pushed me forward in the chow line, forcing me to brush up against the man in front of me. He didn't seem too happy about it.

"You did that on purpose," he accused me.

"I was pushed," I replied.

He took a good look at me and asked, "Are you an Indian?"

"I'm a Menominee Indian."

"I'm McKinney."

"So, you're Irish."

"That's right, and I hate Indians."

"I don't think too much of Irishmen who hate Indians," I told him.

McKinney demanded I meet him after supper and promised, "I'll show you how I can make an Indian cry."

"No white man will ever make me cry!" I replied, rising up to his challenge.

The guy who pushed me announced loudly, "Fight in the boondocks tonight!" That's when I knew he had pushed me on purpose.

I turned to him and said, "You're on my shit list." He laughed in my face. "I'm not worried. When McKinney gets through with you, your ass will be mud." I promised to settle with him later.

A man in our platoon named Bailey heard about the fight and warned me that McKinney* had about ten professional fights to his credit. He said, "Ray, if I can't talk you out of this fight, all I can do is give you a few pointers." He warned me not to go all out in the first part of the fight, keep my guard up, watch for an opening, don't lose my balance, and keep moving. I thought of the time my wolf was being mauled by a bulldog. Kernel had won that fight. I would have to try to be more like him.

After supper, as I walked toward the boondocks, I heard someone yell, "Fight!" I turned to see about twenty men heading my way. By the time I arrived, McKinney was already there.

---

* The names Bailey and McKinney are fictitious, but the events are true to the best of my recollection.

"So, you came to see an Indian cry!" he said, badgering me.

I didn't answer at first and let him badger me some more. Finally I said, "I came here to fight, not talk."

McKinney rushed toward me, but Bailey pushed him back. We took off our dungaree tops and were told to back off. A large circle was drawn for the space we were to fight in. Bailey motioned us to the center and told us the rules. "No hitting below the belt," he said, "and back off once a man is down."

We sparred for a few minutes, and then I took a sharp left to the side of my face. I shook it off and started watching for an opening in McKinney's defense. But he was too sharp to let me get a clean shot at him. He clipped me again and again. I could only let him do the swinging, and I soon noticed that he was getting tired. I was still weak from sick bay, but I had to get this guy, one way or another. Then I got in a good punch, and he shook his head. We threw lefts and rights at each other until I tripped and fell backwards.

When I fell, he kicked me in the ribs and swore at me. Some of the men started to boo him. Then, as I was getting up, Bailey stepped in and said, "No kicking a man when he's down!" He stopped the fight and said to McKinney, "You were getting winded. He would have gotten you if you hadn't kicked him."

My ribs hurt, and I had trouble taking a deep breath. My nose felt broken, too, and that didn't help my breathing. Now I had to go and lick my wounds, just like my wolf. With a broken nose and kicked-in ribs, I had trouble sleeping that night. But when you're eighteen you heal fast.

Bailey came over to my bunk and asked how I was doing. "Nothing a few beers won't fix," I told him. He laughed.

"When we get over boot camp, I'll buy you the best drink in

the house," Bailey promised. Then he added with a faded smile, "The sarge wants to see you in his office." He walked with me to the drill office and waited outside.

Once inside the office, I snapped to attention. "Private Kaquatosh reporting as ordered, sir!"

"Kaquatosh, I hear you've been fist-fighting," the sergeant said.

"No, sir."

"Don't lie to me! I know what's going on in this platoon."

"We were just sparring," I told him.

"Look at your eyes and fists. You call that sparring?"

"We got a little carried away, sir."

"McKinney is a professional boxer."

"I know, sir. He's teaching me how to box."

"He kicked you when you fell. You call that boxing?"

"Yes, sir. That taught me not to fall down."

"I could have McKinney put in the brig for six months for what he did to you."

"Then no one will teach me how to box, sir."

"Are all Indians like you, Kaquatosh?"

"No, sir. They're better fighters than me."

"Go back to your quarters. No more fighting!"

I stepped back one step, did an about-face, and got the hell out of there. Outside, Bailey was laughing his ass off. "You sure told the sarge a good line, but I'm sure he knows better," he said. "Come on over to the gym. I want you to meet a friend of mine."

In the gym was a sergeant instructing some men. He turned and said to me, "I hear you had a fight with a pro."

I smiled and told him, "It wasn't much of a fight. I had better ones on the reservation."

Then Bailey added, "He's a damn good fist-fighter." The sergeant looked at Bailey and said, "They're the best kind." He pointed to a punching bag and said, "Give him all the help he needs, and if you need anything, just ask."

That was the start of my training: skipping rope, shadow boxing, punching a big body bag. This was going to be fun.

But I had a lot to learn. Bailey weighed about two hundred pounds and knew more about boxing than anyone I ever met. He kept telling me to keep my head down so no punches could get to my chin. After a while, my ribs felt no pain, and I was able to go through two rounds of fighting and not get winded. Not too bad for a quiet little Indian. There were times I felt like I could take on Joe Louis, the world boxing champion. Then Bailey would tell me, "Don't get cocky!"

He also warned me, "Look out for McKinney!"

"You got that wrong," I replied. "McKinney has to look out for me."

31

Born to Fight

Bailey trained me for about a month. Now I was looking forward to the next fight.

I didn't have to wait long. One day while standing in the chow line, I heard someone say, "I feel like kicking the shit out of an Indian."

I turned to reply. "That sounds like an Irishman who likes to kick a man when he's down."

"Meet me in the boondocks after chow!" McKinney snapped.

This time someone had brought two small stools from the gym for us to sit on between rounds, and it seemed like the whole platoon was there to watch. McKinney must have been planning for this all afternoon. The only thing he didn't plan on was a referee. Bailey informed him that he would referee the fight. "Any kicking a man when he's down will be considered a win for the man being kicked," Bailey warned. "Shake hands and come out fighting."

McKinney refused. I smiled and said, "What makes you think I'd let you?" That did it.

McKinney took a swing at me, and Bailey grabbed him and pushed him away. Then the bell rang, and McKinney charged into me like a raging bull. I had to back up as he kept swinging like it was the last round. I blocked every one of his punches. Soon he was showing signs of exhaustion. He seemed to grow worried as the end of the round came near.

At the beginning of the second round, I got in a few hits, nothing serious, but then my big break came. McKinney threw a hard right, missed, and gave me the opening I was waiting for. I connected with a hard right to his left eye. He started to bleed. Now it was my turn to throw a few hard punches.

The cut above his left eye was leaking blood, and he kept wiping at it. Each time he did, I connected with a hit. My fist was getting smeared with blood.

In the third round, we sparred for a while, and then I connected with a left cross to McKinney's nose. His head jerked back, and I knew I had hurt him. His nose started to bleed. Then McKinney walked into a stiff right and fell backwards. Bailey came over to start the count.

"Come on, fight, Irishman!" I yelled.

The round was nearly over. Bailey raised his hands, and I knew it was time to give this guy all I had. I peppered him with lefts and rights, and he did the same to me. We stood eye to eye, throwing everything we had at each other. Then we stopped. McKinney staggered, and I thought that this time he would fall, but then he came at me again. As I blocked his punches, I remembered how my wolf stood on his hind legs when he was fighting for his life. Now it was my turn to do the same. So with all my strength, I threw a hard right and connected with the side of McKinney's face. He went down and didn't get back up. The timer sounded, and Bailey came between us.

"Fight's over!" Bailey cried. He held up my arm, and the crowd applauded. Then he walked over to McKinney, who was just standing up, and raised his arm to more applause. Bailey looked at me and said, "Seems like this fight is a draw." He turned to McKinney and asked, "What do you think about that?"

"If it's okay with the Indian . . . ," he replied. Bailey turned to face me with the same question.

"If it's okay with the Irishman, it's okay with me," I smiled.

On the way back to the tent area, Bailey said, "You worked him over pretty good. Did you see that big cut on his left eyebrow?"

"He must have run into someone's fist—three times," I said. Bailey smiled ear to ear.

I knew it was just a matter of time before the sergeant would hear about the fight. The next morning while we were lined up for inspection, the sarge approached me, took a good, long look at my face, lowered his eyes to my knuckles, and said, "Kaquatosh, you've been fighting again. You and McKinney will see me in my office after drill!"

"Yes, sir!"

When drill practice was over, I walked over to the sarge's office and found McKinney standing at attention in front of the desk. "At ease, both of you," said the sergeant. He looked at me and asked, "Private Kaquatosh, can you tell me why Private McKinney's face looks like it went through a meat grinder?"

"Yes, sir," I answered. "He was teaching me how to box, and he fell forward into my fists."

"McKinney, do you agree with that?"

"Yes, sir," answered McKinney, "that's what happened."

The sergeant asked, "Private McKinney, why did you fight with Private Kaquatosh in the first place?"

"Because I hate Indians, sir."

"That will get you thirty days in the brig."

"Sir," I said, "you better give me thirty days as well, because I hate Irishmen."

The sergeant stood up and pushed some papers toward me. "I want you to sign these papers so I can court-martial McKinney for using his professional tactics on you."

"I refuse to do that, sir."

"Give me one good reason why you won't sign a complaint."

"No one can teach me how to box like he can."

At that the sergeant dismissed us with a warning, saying, "No more fighting, or I'll get you both thirty days in the brig on bread and water."

Once we were outside, McKinney looked at me and said, "You have got to be the dumbest Indian in the world."

He didn't faze me. "Just because I let you off the hook doesn't mean I like Irishmen," I replied.

"I still hate Indians," he said.

"Too bad. Indians were born to fight. That's why they call us warriors."

McKinney just hung his head and slowly walked away.

I wondered what was going to happen now that I had gotten McKinney out of my hair. Sometimes after that I would see him in the pay or chow lines, but he would never say anything to me. Maybe he really did hate Indians.

I don't really hate Irishmen, just the ones that tick me off. In my observation, an Irishman is extremely lucky, drinks heavily, will tell you he's Irish within five minutes, takes unnecessary risks, is boastful, likes to fight, and is stubborn—all attributes similar to my own.

32

Sharpshooter

Boot camp was almost over, and we were all looking forward to reporting to the rifle range, where we would get to fire the M-1 rifle and earn a medal. The Expert medal was the number one, Sharpshooter medal number two, and the Marksman medal the lowest you could get.

For the first week, all we did was snapping in: aim, pull the trigger, and make believe you fired. We did the same with the carbine rifle and the Colt 45. Later, we even got to throw a few dummy hand grenades. It grew tiresome after a while.

But by the second week, everyone was excited. We were all set to fire the M-1. When the big day came we were told to lie down on any space numbered from one to fourteen. No one else would take the space for target number thirteen, so I took it.

The target was two hundred yards away. We were given a clip full of ammunition and told to fire at will and call every shot. The ring around the bull's-eye was number one. The second ring was number two and the third number three. If you missed the target, you'd get "Maggie's drawers" (a flag would be raised with a black cloth on it). The top of the target was twelve o'clock, the bottom six o'clock, the right side three o'clock, and the left side nine o'clock. With our arms in the slings of the rifle, we waited for the signal. "Ready on the right? Ready on the left? All ready on the firing line. Commence fire!"

I squeezed off my first shot, calling, "Number one, twelve o'clock!" I continued shooting my way around the outer and inner circles. Then I heard someone holler, "Pinwheel, number thirteen!" *Hey, that's me!*

"Do you know what a pinwheel is?" the sergeant asked me.

"No," I answered.

"It's a bulls-eye. Number thirteen, you're to report to the tower."

I climbed the ladder up the tower, and there stood a full colonel. "Private Kaquatosh reporting as ordered, sir," I said.

The colonel offered me his hand. "Private Kaquatosh, I'd like to shake your hand. Congratulations."

"Thank you, sir."

"Get some more if you can."

"I'll try, sir."

Once again, I nailed it. My number was called, and I was told the colonel wanted to see me again. When I got up to the tower, the colonel was smiling. "Private Kaquatosh, you just made Sharpshooter," he told me.

Everything was going along smoothly, so I knew I had better watch out for the unexpected. I didn't have to wait long.

33

Grudge Fight

On the way back to our living quarters, I met Bailey. "Ray, I've been looking all over for you," he said. "Your name is on the bulletin board over by the gym. You're listed for a grudge fight with McKinney. We got 'til seven tonight."

I told Bailey that McKinney and I had told the sergeant we wouldn't fight anymore. "That was back at the base," Bailey informed me. "Here at the rifle range he has no jurisdiction." In fact, it seemed that grudge fights were encouraged on the rifle range. The only requirement was that we had to use boxing gloves.

After supper, we headed over to the gym. McKinney was working out with a sparring partner. While he was in the ring, I sat and waited for him to finish. When the round was over, McKinney came to the side of the ring and said, "Hey, the Indian finally made it." Then he called out to Bailey: "You won't be referee this time. My friend will."

"I'll keep an eye on him," said Bailey.

"Do that!" McKinney replied. "He'd like to kick your ass."

On the way out, I asked Bailey, "How many rounds?"

"From what I can gather, three. But I'll make sure later."

"Well, that I can do standing on my head."

"Don't get cocky, Ray!"

There would be five fights that night. Ours was the last. Some-one had put on the bulletin board INDIAN VS. IRISH, and this drew in a lot of officers from the bases nearby, both Army and Navy.

Just before the fight, Bailey gave me some final instructions: "With a fist fight you can last longer, but with gloves on you can take more punches. Don't leave yourself open under any circum-stances. Always remember, he has more practice than you. Also, he's been working out since he got here."

I told him, "I appreciate everything you have done for me, and I'll never forget it. Even if I lose, I'll be grateful."

After the fourth fight was over, we entered the ring. He pulled the ropes apart so I could squeeze through. I felt like a king.

McKinney's friend had been disqualified as a referee. When the new referee held up McKinney's arm, he received a big round of applause. Then when the referee came over to my corner and held up my arm, I was announced as the challenger. No wonder McKinney got the loud applause.

McKinney came out of his corner like he was going for the world championship. He danced around like a ballerina. He'd take a punch, back off, and bob and weave. *Play it like a pro,* I kept telling myself. So I kept backtracking and didn't get hit until the end of the round, when he let go with a flurry of punches. I'd been hit harder by one of my ex-girlfriends, so I just laughed it off.

At the start of the second round, I still felt like I could go a full five rounds and not get tired. I watched and let him make his move. There it came: a long right aimed at my left eye. I backed off just enough to throw a left uppercut to his face. A perfect hit. That dazed him. Bailey gave me the signal to follow through, so I rushed forward and gave him a left to the face, then a hard right to his left eye. That did it. He let his guard down just long enough for me to get a left and a hard right to his left eye. He staggered and fell forward. The referee made me go back to my corner.

At the end of the round, Bailey was smiling like the lumber-jacks did when they walked out of a whorehouse. McKinney wasn't coming out so fast for round three, but I remembered not to be cocky. I sidestepped his first punch and countered with a hard right to the left side of his face. That made him stagger a bit. He regained his balance. I thought he'd had enough, so I backed off. Then I asked myself, *What am I doing? This is the man who's out to get me!* I rushed toward him and threw a left and right—both missed. Then I got lucky and connected with a hard right that made him turn toward the ropes, just in time for me to get him with a stiff left, followed by a hard right to the face, sending him back against the ropes. He fell forward on his face. I had knocked him out. The referee motioned me toward my corner.

McKinney couldn't get up. I thought I had killed him. As I was going over to his corner, Bailey stopped me. At the same time, the referee stopped the fight. Bailey was smiling and crying at the same time. "You did it! You did it!" he exclaimed.

"How does my face look?" I asked.

"Beautiful. Not a scratch on it."

"How's McKinney?"

"To hell with him!"

As Bailey was untying my gloves, he started to laugh and said, "Don't fuck with the Indian!" We laughed so hard, tears came to my eyes.

The next day, we boarded a bus to return to boot camp for our new assignments: tank corps, aviation, cooking school, or another branch of the Marine Corps. We were no longer considered "boots"—we were new Marines.

We lined up for roll call. When the sergeant got to my name, he said, "Private Kaquatosh, report to the Officer of the Day at 1300."

"I'm coming with you," Bailey said.

After lunch, we walked over to the office. We entered, and I said, "Private Kaquatosh reporting as ordered, sir."

"At ease, Private Kaquatosh," said the O.D. Sitting beside him was our old drill sergeant. "You had a fight at the rifle range last night?"

"Yes, sir."

"Tell me about it."

"They put my name on the bulletin board when we arrived at the range. I didn't know about it until last night," I told him.

The O.D. asked, "What did the bulletin board say?"

"Grudge fight: Indian versus Irishman."

"All the while you were at the camp you knew nothing about this fight?"

"No, sir. If I had, I would have started training long before last night."

"Did McKinney train while he was at the camp?"

"I don't know."

"You don't know, or you're lying?"

"I mean, I can't say for sure. But when I entered the gym last night, McKinney was sparring with someone."

"Did you win last night?"

The sergeant answered for me. "He KO'd him, sir."

"Sergeant, how many fights has McKinney had?"

"Ten or eleven."

"Private Kaquatosh, will you sign these papers to court-martial McKinney for fighting a nonprofessional man?"

"No, sir. I can't do that to my friend."

"How can he be your friend when he calls you a fuckin' Indian?" asked the sergeant.

"Because I call him a fuckin' Irishman."

"Kaquatosh, because you won't sign these papers, I'm going to have to consider this case closed. Report back to your platoon."

I took one step backwards and saw that the sergeant was smiling. I made an about-face and got out of there before he changed his mind.

34

Assignments

After rifle range training was over and I returned to the Marine Corps base, I had the right to wear my emblems, because I was no longer a "boot." Among other things, this permitted me to enjoy the privilege of going to the beer hall, known as the slop shoot.

Bailey and I agreed to go to early chow, see a movie, and then head to the slop shoot around eleven. While we were standing in the chow line, I felt a slap on my back and heard someone say, "I still hate Indians." Before I turned around, I responded, "That must be that damn Irishman."

When I turned, McKinney held out his hand to shake mine. We both had a good laugh.

Bailey was standing in front of me in line. "McKinney, Ray and I are going to the early movie and then we're going to close the slop shoot."

"Got room for another?" McKinney asked.

"The more the merrier," answered Bailey. "I'm buying the first drink."

McKinney took one look at me and said, "Never argue with a man who's buying."

"I'd be a disgrace to all Indians if I refused," I said.

"That goes for me and all the Irish," McKinney said.

We got to the bar, and the barman asked, "What'll it be?"

I looked at McKinney and answered, "I'll take a case of beer and one for my friend."

The barman looked puzzled and said, "We only sell it by the bottle."

"Oh, great, just when my friend was going to buy," I replied.

After we downed a few beers, we weren't feeling any pain. McKinney asked what had happened at the O.D.'s office. "They wanted me to sign some papers to nail you," I answered.

"You mean, because he's a pro?" asked Bailey.

"That's right, and I told them no, I couldn't do that to my friend. So they said the case was closed."

McKinney almost couldn't believe it. "You dumb Indian," he said, "you had me by the ass, and you didn't sign! I could've been discharged."

Now it all made sense. "So that's why you kept fighting me. I oughta take another punch at that eye," I said.

"Try it!" McKinney challenged.

"Hey, knock it off!" interrupted Bailey. "This is our last day together."

"You think I'm going to miss that damn Irishman?"

"Yeah, just like I'll miss you, damn Indian."

"I'd like to shake both your hands," said Bailey.

"How 'bout it?" I asked McKinney.

"I guess he's right," he replied.

We both shook Bailey's hand, and I said, "I'm buying the next round."

"That's the best news I've ever heard from an Indian," laughed McKinney.

The next morning our eyes looked like pee-holes in the snow. My head felt like McKinney had been pounding on it all night long, but it was the best hangover I ever had.

After roll call, the sergeant called off our names to different branches of the Marines.

"Bailey: infantry! McKinney: aviation! Kaquatosh: tank corps!"

I spoke up: "Sergeant, I'd like to go into aviation."

"That's all filled," he said.

"Sergeant," said McKinney, "I'd like to go into the tank corps."

"Kaquatosh, would you like to change places with McKinney?" the sergeant asked. Then he added, "Well? Are you two talking to each other?"

"Yeah," I answered, "but I still hate Irishmen." McKinney looked at me and said, "Too bad you're an Indian, you'd make a good Irish fighter."

"We Indians are already warriors."

The sergeant walked over to us and said, "I'd like to shake both your hands. I'm going to miss you two. Now get your asses out of here!"

McKinney was killed in action sometime in 1944. He received the Purple Heart and the Bronze Star. Bailey was also killed in action while he was trying to help someone. He was awarded the Silver Star and Purple Heart. That was Bailey, always trying to help someone, even at his own expense. We will all meet again. It's only a matter of time.

35

Naval Training Center

The first week after boot camp, we were transferred to the Naval Training Center in San Diego. There we had to take a short course on clerical procedures for requisitioning supplies. This detached duty from the Marines was too good to be true. In other words, when everything goes smoothly, look out!

Every day as we marched to the mess hall, we had to pass the "swabbies" (sailors) barracks on each side of the street. On the second floor was a walkway from one building to the other. When the swabbies saw us coming, they would gather on the walkway and spit on us as we walked under it. They knew we couldn't do anything about it, so they kept on, and it frustrated us.

One day I was put in charge of the squad.

"Fall in for chow-call!" I yelled. Everyone formed three ranks and waited for my command. "Have any of you been spit on by the swabbies?" I asked. They all raised their hands. Then I asked, "How would you like to do get even?" They were all in.

About twenty feet from the walkway, I could see the swabbies gathering for their usual spit-on. "Platoon . . . halt! Listen carefully," I said. "When they start spitting, I'll holler 'break.' The left half of the platoon will rush up the left stairs, and the right half will go to the right stairs, and we'll catch them in between. Then it's time to get even. Okay? Here goes!"

As we started to pass under the walkway, they started spitting, and I hollered: "Break!" We caught those swabbies in between the crosswalks. When we were finished, some were sitting on the steps holding their heads or lying down in agony, and some had run away. With no one left to dance with, I hollered, "Fall in!"

Now we headed for the mess hall. "Platoon . . . halt!" Before I dismissed the squad, I said, "I'd like to thank you men for helping me get even with those swabbies. I know the sergeant will have me reprimanded for this, but I'll smile all the way to the brig."

One man said, "If he does, we'll all go with you."

Another one added, "We all volunteered."

Later that afternoon, two security police came looking for me. They wanted to know who was in charge of the squad that had tangled with their men. Three of the guys said, "I was in charge!" Then I stepped forward and said, "Don't listen to them. I was in charge."

"The Officer of the Day would like to talk to you."

They walked me over to the office, and all the men in my squad walked behind us. "Were you in charge of the squad that tangled with our men in the overpass?" asked the O.D.

"Yes, sir."

"Why didn't you stop them from fighting?"

"Because for two weeks they spit on us. I had to wipe their slime off my clothes, and I couldn't take it any longer."

"Why didn't you report this to the security police?" he asked.

"Because I hate to complain," I said.

"So, you'd rather fight than complain."

"No, sir. I hoped it would stop after the first two weeks, but it's been getting worse," I told him.

"Do you realize how badly our men were hurt?"

"No, sir."

"Sick bay reports two broken noses, sprained ankle, cuts, bruises, three black eyes. How 'bout your men?"

"None of them went to sick bay," I told him.

"Have you anything to say to me about this matter?"

"Yes, sir. I'm a proud Marine, and I don't believe any man in service should be spit upon by another serviceman."

"I can promise you that there will be no more spitting, if you can promise me that there will be no more fighting."

"You have my word on that, sir."

"Good. Any more trouble, come see me."

"Thank you, sir."

He dismissed me and wished me good luck. After that, there was no more spitting. Now we could go to the mess hall and not have to wipe slime off our clothes.

36

Overseas

In early August 1943 we were on twenty-four-hour alert, waiting to board a troop ship bound for the South Pacific. One day we were given an hour to have all of our gear loaded on a truck. This truck took us to a troop transport ship docked in the harbor at San Diego. The ship was the *Klip Fontaine,* and it was operated by sailors from the West Indies. They didn't speak English.

One day while I was walking by the sailors' galley, one of them pushed me for no reason. I backed off, but he pushed me again. So I grabbed him by the collar and waist and made believe I was going to throw him overboard. That did it. When I dropped him, he ran squealing back to his galley. Later I happened to meet him at the bow. He looked at me and bowed. I did the same, and he smiled. Now I felt sorry for him, so I offered him a Coke. He grabbed it, smiled, and bit the cap off. After that he would bow and smile whenever he saw me.

Our commanding officer called us for a lecture near the sailors' quarters. As we approached, the sailors were squatting and smoking nearby. When they noticed me, they all got up, put their hands together like they were praying, and bowed to me. I stopped and did the same.

The first day out of port we had smooth sailing, but the next day the ocean became rough. The waves got bigger until the bow of the ship disappeared into them. We were ordered to clear the deck and get below. Hundreds of men became seasick. If the motion didn't get to you, the stench did.

Volunteers were needed for gun watch, so I took a turn. I was taken to portside of the ship and positioned in a turret with twin .50-caliber guns. The guns were loaded and ready to be fired. I was shown how to strap on the shoulder harness and how to activate the guns. Four hours later, I was relieved of my watch and taken down to the crew's mess hall. No more standing in line with the troops. I was now part of the ship's crew.

Everything was going along smoothly, so I knew that something was about to happen. "Attention all personnel, we have a fish on our tail. Be on lookout!"

Sonar had picked up a sub. It was after us. When someone brought me coffee, I asked, "Can we outrun that fish?"

"This old tub can do 25 knots, and the sub can only do about 15," a crewman answered.

"What happens if they surface and try to keep up with us?"

The crewman laughed and replied, "We just shoot the hell out of them. We have enough guns."

The red alert was called off two hours later. My four-hour watch was over, and I returned to the crew's quarters for relaxation and a delicious meal.

After a week at sea, we had reached the southern hemisphere, near the equator. At this latitude, we began to swelter. It was so hot we were given salt tablets to prevent dehydration.

Each day I welcomed the night, when my turret seemed cool compared to the rest of the ship.

Late one night, the phone buzzed: "Number 10 gunner, keep your attention on the southern horizon for the Southern Cross off the port bow." A few seconds later, the constellation became visible. I was mesmerized by it. Four stars form a perfect cross, seemingly brighter than the other stars in the sky. We were getting near the end of our voyage. My daydreaming came to a sudden stop when the buzzer sounded: "Number 10 gunner, be on the lookout for escort ships on port bow!" Hey, that's good news. No more subs.

Now that we had the Southern Cross for company, all I had to do was look south and watch for the escorts. Just after dark one night, I looked at the horizon and saw a tiny object that flashed a light. I grabbed the phone and reported it. A few seconds later a crewman phoned me. "Number 10, good show. We have an escort."

It took two weeks to reach New Caledonia. When we started to disembark, some of my West Indian pals showed up. I slowly walked over to them and handed each of them a pack of cigarettes. As I shook their hands, they seemed very happy. Once I got on dock, I looked up and saw that they were waving. One of my friends noticed and said, "Why did they seem sad?" I looked at him and said, "Because they respected me. I was nice to them."

That same afternoon, we embarked on a Navy ship and were transported farther north, to a supply area at the New Hebrides Islands. This was an island paradise, something you would see only in movies about the South Pacific. There were palm trees, coconut, banana, lemon, and orange trees. We had small huts to live in, and there was even an airfield.

And now the bad news. In the hot weather, we had to consume a lot of water. I dipped my canteen cup in a bucket, took a taste, and spit it out. The water was mixed with chlorine. But we had to drink it or dehydrate. The food was almost as bad: dehydrated potatoes, milk, eggs, and fruit. What could be worse? Mutton, that's what! They fried it, baked it, put it in a stew, and it still had an awful taste. The Navy Seabees and the Army, who also had bases nearby, had the best food. What they didn't want, they gave to us. We would have to endure these deplorable conditions for over a year.

One day I felt cold even though the temperature outside was well over 90 degrees. I started to shake and couldn't stop. Next I was so hot that sweat was pouring off my forehead. Then I felt cold again. Sick bay recorded my temperature at 105. They transported me to the naval hospital at other end of the island. Diagnosis: malarial fever.

At first I thought I was going to die, but after a while I didn't care. I couldn't eat or sleep. My head hurt terribly. Then one morning I was awakened by an angel. I looked up to see a nice-looking nurse.

"Are you an angel, or am I dreaming?" I asked.

She smiled.

"How long have I been here?"

"About a week.

I tried to move and couldn't. I looked at her and said, "I can't lift my arm."

"That's because you haven't had anything to eat," she said. "How about some ice cream?"

"First I'd like some water. My mouth tastes like some seagulls scored a direct hit in it."

The nurse smiled and handed me a glass of water, but I was too weak to lift the glass, so she lifted my head and poured a little down my throat.

When I arrived at this place, I weighed 165 pounds, but by the time I got out, I was down to about 150. I had to make new notches in my belt, and my shirt felt loose. For the rest of my life I would stay at 150 pounds, give or take a few. I know this illness affected my metabolism. Sometimes I have flashbacks: I begin to shiver, then the sweat starts to form on my forehead, and I become weak. After a little while, I begin to feel better.

After another week I was back loading ships and planes with supplies. We were never out of work, and sometimes we worked all night. While I worked, I enjoyed watching the planes land and take off. I saw all kinds of aircraft—Corsair F4Us, SBD Dauntless dive bombers, some old F4Fs. The most common was the DC-3 cargo ship. We called it the workhorse of WWII.

Then, just when we were getting used to the island, we heard we were going to be put on alert to go into action. We were ordered to move the supplies stored around our hut area to the docks, ready for loading. This was bad news. All the time I was stationed on this island, I hadn't gotten to hitch a ride on any of the aircraft. Now that we were on alert, my hopes of getting to fly dimmed.

37

Peleliu Island, Palau

In September 1944 General Douglas MacArthur was about to make good on his promise to the Philippine people: "I shall return." But he needed a little help from the Marines.

The island of Peleliu, Palau, about five hundred miles southeast of the Philippines, had to be taken. This was our destination. The Marines had already landed and had the situation well in hand, or so we thought. We were assigned to our bunks aboard the destroyer that was to take us to Peleliu and given some instructions about the ship's operation. When we got underway, I decided to make some inquiries about the gun watches. I learned they needed men to keep watch on the starboard side of the ship.

The first night out, we ran into bad weather. All the hatches had to be secured, and topside had to be cleared at all times. The ship's crew told us to prepare for the worst. The escort ships disappeared behind huge waves, and all we could see of them was the flag on top of the mast. Each time our ship plowed into the waves, the bow disappeared and water came all the way to the middle of the ship. The men in our outfit and even some of the ship's crew started to get sick. They said it was the worst storm they had ever encountered. The smell was so terrible. I was glad I was on gun watch. I had to be strapped in so I wouldn't be washed overboard.

After I had endured four hours of this, my replacement stumbled into the turret, soaking wet, and said, "Watch the waves. When the ship's bow comes out, make a break for the door, and be sure and secure it after you enter!"

Finally we docked in Finchhaven, New Guinea. The Navy boys picked us up in one of their warships. It was a destroyer, and this gave me a hint that we were heading for action.

When we docked at Manus Island, we saw the ravages of war. The coconut trees were blown down, and the earth was black from fire. I was glad to get back to the ship. We cleared the port of Manus, and on the way to Peleliu we heard what sounded like thunder. It was warships engaging in battle.

Now we could see smoke billowing up above Peleliu. The Navy was doing a good job on the ridges, mountains, and beaches. We docked on Orange Beach, and the Navy "weasels" (amphibious vehicles) were ready to take us ashore.

With a full pack on my back, a rifle, and a duty belt with a Colt 45 strapped on my side, I was ready to go ashore. We had to climb down a rope ladder draped over the side of the ship. The weasel bobbed up and down with each wave. A man just below me tried to jump into the weasel, but he got pinned against the ship and broke his leg. I tried to help him, but he fell before I could get to him. Now it was my turn. I waited until the weasel rose close to me, and then I jumped right into it. The guy with the broken leg was moaning in pain. I took his pack off, placed it under his leg, gave it a little pull, and straightened it out. The weasel took him back to the ship.

We hit the beach. To my surprise, there were no Japanese waiting. Green trucks were ready to transport us to the airport. We climbed aboard. "Keep your heads down while I transport you to the base," we were told. "We're heading into sniper area."

As we rode along, we got a whiff of a rotten odor. I knew what it was: decomposing human flesh. The odor grew stronger as we neared the base. The driver stopped the truck and pointed to an area about fifty yards away. "Your new home," he said. We walked toward the tent area, and I tripped and fell. I came face to face with a skull. I had tripped on a shoe that still had a foot in it. Japanese bodies lay all around us, with huge flies swarming all over them. I couldn't believe it. I wondered why they didn't bury them. I soon found out: we had hardly enough time to bury our own. I know, because I had to do the burying many times.

A whiz went past my head. I thought it was a bee. Then I heard the pop. *Hey, those dirty dogs are shooting at us,* I thought.

The stench was unbearable, making it hard to breathe without wretching. I didn't eat for the rest of the day. But hunger knows no shame, and I would have to eat or starve.

Still weak from hunger and malaria, I was put on grave detail. They asked for volunteers: "You, you, you, and the Indian." As I buried the men, I never shed a tear. Remember, no white man will ever make me cry. I just kept thinking about these men, and I knew they would have done the same if they were in my shoes.

Our tent area was located next to the airstrip. This was the place we would call home for the next two months. It was also close to the sniper area. Each night, the Japanese would sneak out of the caves and wait until daylight to shoot at us with their telescopic rifles.

As darkness fell on this tropical hellhole, we saw the first flare go up and slowly turn night into day as it parachuted down. Then we could see the tracer bullets being fired toward the caves. The sound of grenades and the bark of Browning automatic rifles could be heard all night. I never slept a wink until daybreak, for fear of getting bayoneted by the suicide Japanese who got through the front lines.

War is hell on earth. With the temperature well over 110 degrees, we had to drink a lot of water and take salt tablets to retain it. The water reeked of chlorine, but I forced myself to drink it. I reminded myself I was a Marine and thought if the white men could tolerate it, so could I.

The daytime heat was unbearable. Flies feasted on the dead and also tried to eat the living. With sweat dripping from our foreheads and constantly trying to keep the flies from biting, we could work for only a little while at a time. Almost every day, we had to bury the men killed on the ridges. Their dogtags were still on them. We removed one, tacked it on a small white cross, and left the other tag with the body as we wrapped it in a blanket and covered it with sand. As we did, I thanked the Great Spirit for letting me live one more day.

It got to be routine watching the tracers fly toward the caves at night, the flares floating down, and the *rat-a-tat-tat* of machine gun fire. The banzai (suicide) attacks were always a threat. After dark we used a password: "Amarillo." It seemed the Japanese couldn't pronounce this word. Anyone entering your tent had to say the word or risk getting shot. I never slept a wink. I just waited for the tent flap to fly open. If someone came in without giving the password, they'd be history.

We lived from day to day, never knowing who would be next. One day someone told me that one of our men got it. They told me he saw it coming. He opened his mouth when he saw the sniper, and the bullet went through his mouth and out his neck. His neck was broken. It was events like this that made us hate to get close to one another personally, for fear of being devastated when someone you knew well got killed. And so we remained aloof.

There were some very cold men in our outfit. One day while we were burying someone, one of the men said, "When you get killed, can I have your wristwatch?" That jolted me to reality.

I answered, "Sure, and if you get killed first, can I have your gold teeth?"

"Why, you dirty bastard," he snapped back, "you'd take my teeth just to get even."

"Don't mess with the Indian!" one of the other men warned. We all laughed.

In a combat area, you become jittery, you get frigid, or you become just plain scared. The sound of gunshot makes you duck for cover all the time. Some men referred to this as combat fatigue. But you can't afford to take chances.

Something else I learned: never volunteer. When you volunteer, something bad always happens. On most of these jobs, they volunteered for me. Again it was, "You, you, you, and the Indian." I soon got sick of that.

On the way back from supper one night, a man in the tent next to ours asked, "Can you help me with this?" After taking a close look at what he held in his hand, I backed off. Seems he was a little curious about the functions of a hand grenade. He had taken it apart and held the detonator in his hand. I hollered, "Don't release it!" He didn't listen. It blew off two of his fingers. He started to scream, so I grabbed his hand and wrapped it in a cloth. A corpsman took him to sick bay.

I was glad he hadn't tried to dissect a landmine.

38

Prank

There are two types of Marines I never wanted to serve with: the pranksters and the curious. Either one can get you killed or put you in sick bay.

About a month after we arrived at Peleliu, we were told a movie was going to be shown after dark. We all looked forward to some entertainment. A screen was set up in front of the mess hall's slop trench. Coconut logs were laid in rows for seating, and some empty oil drums were placed along the rows of logs.

Just before the movie started, I noticed some guys playing tricks on their buddies. They were laughing and having a good time.

It was a moonless night, and it was so dark that when the movie stopped I had to light a match to see the guy next to me. The pranksters decided to give one of their buddies a real jolt by putting half a can of gunpowder under his butt. They put a can on top of the powder, waited until the film reel had to be changed, and then one of them threw a match. The powder went off with a WHAM.

Someone hollered, "Grenade!"

We were all gun-shy, and the least little pow or bang made us all duck for cover. Now everyone ran in all directions. The base doctor flew right through the movie screen and into the slop trench behind it. Then the empty oil drums started to roll, and someone hollered, "Tanks!"

More men jumped into the slop trench with the doctor. I kept hollering, "False alarm, false alarm!" But by the time I got anyone to listen to me, it was too late. The damage had been done. The doctor had ruined the screen. There would be no movies for a long time.

The next morning, the line at the sick bay tent was longer than the chow line. When the doc came limping in, he appeared in worse shape than some of the men. My malaria pills were getting low, so I waited at the tent until the last man came out.

The doc motioned to me to enter. I told him, "The next time you have to go to the head, don't jump through the movie screen!"

"You were there, eh?" he said.

"Yes, I was the one who kept hollering 'False alarm!'"

"What can I do for you?" he asked.

"Don't jump through the movie screen. Oh, and you could give me some pills for malaria."

He gave me the medicine and said, "Tell me what happened last night."

"Some men were playing tricks on their buddies. They put gunpowder under a can, put a match to it, and it blew up like a grenade. You know the rest."

"I'd like to get my hands on those S.O.Bs," he said.

"No need to. I turned them in to the colonel. He's going to send them up to the front lines on the ridge. They'll hear a lot of grenades and tanks up there." Then I asked, "So, how many Purple Hearts were given out?"

"We all could use one," the doctor replied.

39

Thanksgiving 1944

In November the temperature was well over 115 degrees on Pele-liu. Scuttlebutt was that President Roosevelt had promised that all troops fighting on various fronts would get a turkey dinner for Thanksgiving this year. How could they keep turkey fresh in this kind of heat? I had never heard of canned turkey, but I was about to.

The chow line was unusually long. I hurried to get in line and inadvertently stepped in front of a full colonel. I said, "Sorry, sir. I didn't see your emblems."

He replied, "Stay right where you are, corporal. In combat, we officers eat with the enlisted men. Don't salute me. And knock off the sir!"

The colonel appeared exhausted and needed a shave. His attire was soiled with dirt and sweat.

"Been up on the ridge?" I asked.

"How did you guess?"

More than five hundred Marines were killed taking this expensive piece of real estate. They had named it Bloody Nose Ridge and erected a huge white cross on it. I had just missed that action. How lucky could I get?

We moved slowly along the line, and the cooks threw the food at us. One was tossing the dinner rolls, and he never missed a tray.

He could have pitched for the Yankees. Another cook placed the turkey carefully on my tray like a surgeon using forceps. It looked the same as the turkey at home. I couldn't believe all this food was for me. We even had cranberry sauce. At the end of the line was a big vat of coffee. I dipped my canteen cup in and filled it to the brim. Now all I had to do was find a place to eat. I spotted an oil drum and rushed to put my tray on it. Then I heard someone say, "Got room for another?"

I turned and said, "Sure." It was the colonel.

We had to keep one hand constantly moving over our food to keep the flies off. One fly got too close to my dinner roll, and as I took a swat at it, I missed and knocked my roll off the tray. As I reached for it, the colonel said, "Remember, no seconds." So I dusted it off and took a bite. As I chewed it, I could feel the sand crunch with every bite. Who cares? A little sand never hurt anyone.

Another fly got too close to my coffee, and I knocked it into my cup. When I flipped it out, I looked at the colonel and said, "I know, no seconds." He smiled, and we kept waving the flies off. When we finished and parted, the colonel waved to me. I remembered not to salute him.

The wind shifted, and we got that awful stench from the rotting bodies. I was grateful we had had enough time to finish this meal in peace. Afterwards, I was ordered to take three men and pick up some equipment on the other side of the island. En route we observed a Seabee plowing a trench. His tractor would disappear in the trench, and all we could see was the black smoke from the exhaust pipe until he emerged at the other end. When we got closer, I noticed he had some sort of cloth over his nose. Then I saw the bodies stacked near the trench. Now I knew where all the flies and stench were coming from. After the Seabee plowed the trench, he turned his tractor around and pushed the bodies into it. The stench still lingered.

The Japanese were a formidable foe. They refused to surrender. I believe they would rather die with honor. Their motto was: "To die for the Emperor is to live forever." The Army took some of them prisoner. We Marines didn't take any. Not long after Thanksgiving, we heard that an officer was killed near the ridge. I hoped it was not the colonel I met at Thanksgiving dinner.

The day they flew me off that island, the stench was still there, along with the chlorine-laced water, K-rations, C-rations, dehydrated potatoes, eggs, milk, and fruit. I miss it like a toothache. Sometimes I wonder if that huge white cross is still on Bloody Nose Ridge.

40

Never Volunteer

After about six weeks in that cesspool, we were getting to feel the strain and pain of war. The handling of dead bodies, grave digging, the stench, chlorinated water, heat, and flies that wouldn't leave us alone—all of it was too much for a quiet little Indian like me.

Finally, good news came. Our time was up, and we were waiting for a ship to take us back home. But there was one more detail, and the sergeant needed four volunteers. "You, you, you, and the Indian. Go pick up two weapons carriers and go to the edge of the ridge and pick up those oil drums. Now!" the sarge ordered. "And don't take any chances!" Did he think we'd be gambling up there?

Then the sarge said, "Kaquatosh, you have a permit to operate a weapons carrier. You'll be the driver." *Yeah, thanks for nothing,* I thought.

With the sun beating down on my helmet, it felt like I had put my head in a blast furnace. We strapped on our Colt 45s, grabbed a carbine, and headed for the oil drum site. No one wanted to crawl on top of the oil drums, which were piled four rows up. This was sniper territory. Our time was up, and nobody wanted to get shot at.

"Ray, you're in charge of this detail, get up there!" said one.

"Okay, but you better be ready when I push them off!" I said.

Never volunteer. "One more to go, here it comes!" I pushed the drum off and stood up. Then I felt a sting on my right ankle, and my foot seemed to buckle underneath me. At that moment, we heard the BANG! By that time, you know it's too late. A sniper hit me on the leg.

They drove me back to the base, and a corpsman took me to the tent hospital on the other side of the island. On the way to the hospital, we had to go through some sniper areas. "That's all I need, more snipers," I thought.

Someone helped me cut the strings off my shoe, and the corpsman gave me a shot to numb the pain. X-rays revealed a fractured fibula. The docs put my leg in a cast up to my knee and sent me to a ward in one of the tents. I was the only one there on crutches. The man on one side of me couldn't talk. The one on the other side had shrapnel embedded in his back. He couldn't move to get his water, so I helped him, holding the curved glass tube in his water cup toward his mouth.

The chief surgeon in charge of this tent hospital, a Navy captain, came in to give us a lecture. His voice shook, and he screamed at us. He had been at this hospital since the invasion, and he was about to crack up. "There'll be no cussing or using four-letter words. You are now under the protection of the United States Navy. You are not allowed to have any weapons . . ."

Great, there goes my 45, I thought.

"Anyone who violates these rules will be thrown out. There is no smoking. If you don't take your medication, you'll be thrown out. Your meals will be brought to you. Don't waste any food."

His voice started to shake more, and I could see tears forming in his eyes. I knew he was under a lot of strain, and I felt sorry for him. He'd had the chance to go home, but he refused to leave his patients. That's what I call dedication.

War seemed to bring out the best in us, as well as the worst.

When his lecture was over, someone took my gun from me. Then I turned to the patient near me. His told me his name was Bob, and he was from Indiana. "What's wrong with you?" I asked.

"Nothing a couple of beers won't fix," he answered. I knew he was lying.

"I'll see what I can do for you," I promised. "How long you been here?"

"About a week."

"They gonna cut on ya?" I asked.

"No, they say it's too close to my heart."

"They just put my ankle in a cast," I said.

"You got a gun?"

"No. Why?"

"Those dirty Japs are picking us off one by one at night."

"What about the corpsman? He has a gun."

"They usually pick him off first. They've got two while I've been here."

"I'll see about getting one of my friends to smuggle me in a 45," I offered.

"Good. Then maybe we can get some sleep."

"Wake me if you need anything."

Bob fell asleep and didn't move until the next morning. A few times that night, I couldn't see him breathing, and I thought he was dead. The doctors came in and stood around him, deciding how and where to operate. "Too risky," one said. Some of them just shook their heads.

A couple friends dropped in to see how I was doing. They said, "We'll be getting a beer ration in tomorrow." Now that was good news! As they were leaving, I said, "Don't forget to bring me a 45 with two clips of ammo."

The next day one of the men slipped me a 45 and asked, "What kind of place is this?" I told him I was under the protection of the US Navy, and no guns were allowed. Still, the corpsmen were being bumped off and no one cared. "Get out of here, fast!" My friend said. Then he smiled and asked: "Do they allow beer in here?" This made me laugh. He handed me a bag with four cans of Pabst inside. After he left, I buried the cans in the sand under my cot.

A few days later, I asked the guy who couldn't talk if he could drink a beer. His eyes seemed to glow, and he nodded his head as if to say yes. My friends knew I couldn't open a can of beer without an opener, so they had taped one to a can. All I had to do was pop it open without letting any of the other patients hear it. Then I borrowed one of Bob's glass tubes so my fellow patient could drink out of it. His hands were shaking as I handed it to him. I told him to sip it slowly. He did, sighed, and handed it back to me.

"Are you okay?" I asked. He nodded. I wrapped the can in some paper and handed it back to him. He looked surprised because I hadn't taken a drink. "It's all yours," I said to him. Then I told him to take his time and not let the corpsman see it.

So there we sat, both smiling, and then something wonderful happened. He spoke.

"Thanks," he said very slowly. It was the first word I heard from him in over a week. He finished the whole can. I told him not to talk, get some rest, and wake me if he needed anything. He smiled and dozed off.

As Bob slept, the corpsman called to me, "Ray, get your ass over to the doc's office!"

The doctor told me to sit. Then he pulled a knife out of the scabbard he had fastened to his belt. He started to make a groove in my cast. He said to the corpsman, "Take the thermometer out of his mouth before he bites it in half!"

"Better get me some skivvies, too," I added, "in case I shit in mine."

The doctor and corpsman started to laugh. All the while they were cutting my cast off, they laughed. Finally the doc grabbed each side of the cast and broke it loose from my ankle. What a relief! Now I could scratch away the dead skin.

When they told me I could leave, I asked about the man next to me who didn't speak. They told me to help him drink plenty of water to help his vocal chords heal, and soon he should start talking.

"How long do I have to stay here?" I asked.

"Anytime you feel you can stand on that foot or walk, you'll be discharged," they answered.

With three cans of Pabst Blue Ribbon beer under my bed, I wanted to get back and help the guy who couldn't talk. He seemed happy to see me. I dug out a can of beer and pointed to the can, then his mouth. He nodded, so I popped the can open and handed it to him. He handed it back to me, but I refused and told him, "It's all for you."

I told him to take his time, and then he slowly said, "I really am glad to meet you."

We sat there smiling at each other. I told him my name was Ray. Then I asked him what his name was. I made him take another drink, and he answered, "Joe."

With a watering mouth, I watched Joe drink the whole can. I knew he needed it more than I did, so I had to suffer a little. Who cares? I found out Joe was an Italian from Chicago. I never knew his last name, but I knew he'd always remember that can of Pabst beer and the Indian who gave it to him.

With Joe on the mend, I felt better. Now all we had to do was get Bob on the road to recovery. He slept most of the time, and they had to give him morphine to ease his pain. The flies tried to land on him, and I kept brushing them off. I'd cover his arms whenever I had to leave him.

Because I had suffered only a slight wound, I was eager to get out. There were too many with more serious wounds, and I felt like I was depriving them of much-needed care. But my ankle hurt so much. I couldn't put much weight on it, let alone walk. Finally I managed to limp around, and I discarded my crutches.

My last night in that tent of suffering was the most memorable. Bob woke from his long sleep and asked for a drink of water. "I don't have any water, but I have a can of Pabst," I told him. As he tried to get up, he said, "No shit!" Then he added, "I haven't had a beer in two months." With two cans of beer left, I knew Bob needed one before his surgery. So I popped the can, put his glass tube in it, and held it while he took a long sip. He said, "Wow, that's the best beer I've had in my whole life."

When he finished drinking, I asked, "How's the pain?"

"What pain?" he answered. Then he said, "Ray, I'm getting drunk."

"Good," I replied. "I got one more can for you."

Bob fell asleep still clutching the beer. I slowly removed the can from his hand and placed it under his bed. Then I remembered to pour a little on the ground. Some of us Indians believe that to do this is to honor the spirits, and they will smile on you.

The doctors in this tent hospital did their major surgery late at night, perhaps because during the day it was too hot and there were too many flies. They had Bob's operation scheduled for this night.

During my stay, I had kept my eye on the corpsman, hoping he wouldn't get hurt or killed. On this night, as the corpsman was turning down the lantern, the tent flap flew open. He dropped the lantern, and it went out. He never made a sound. There were three shots, then an eerie silence like I had never experienced before. I could feel my heart pounding as I sat on my bed wondering if the corpsman was all right. Maybe we were under attack by some suicide Japanese. Maybe I'd be next. Fear engulfed me as I sat there clutching my 45. I knew we didn't stand a chance, but I reached for the clips of ammunition and waited . . . and waited. I was sure we were going to be killed. My first thought was to kill as many as possible.

Bob broke the silence and asked, "How many did you get?" My answer was short. "None." Then I told him, "The corpsman got both of them." I was still hiding the fact that I had a 45.

He didn't believe me. "You're lying, Ray." We could hear voices, and I thought we were under attack again. I told Bob to be quiet. The voices got louder, and I breathed a sigh of relief when I heard someone say, "Over here." The doctors and corpsmen were swarming all over the place. I told Bob to pretend he was sleeping.

Later that night, the doctors came for Bob. Just before they took him away, I said, "I've got another can of beer, and when you get back we'll have a little party." He reached for my hand and held it so tightly they had to pull us apart. All night long I waited, but they never brought him back.

Before breakfast, someone came in and rolled up his mattress. When they rolled up your mattress, it meant that you were done for. Damn it! Joe woke up and saw that Bob's mattress was rolled up. When he saw me sitting with my head hanging down, he made an effort to talk, and that might have been a good thing. He managed to say: "I'm sorry."

"Your voice sounds better," I said. "That beer did it. The power of alcohol!"

We sat there laughing.

We lived from day to day, never knowing who would be next. Bob was here last night, now he was gone. I thanked the Great Spirit for letting me live one more day. Now I asked him to take care of Bob.

Later I hopped over to the new corpsman's desk. He appeared fresh out of grade school. He asked, "What can I do for you?"

I asked, "When's Bob coming back?"

The corpsman didn't answer, so I asked him again. He looked at me with tears forming in his eyes and yelled, "Do I have to spell it out for you?" Then, with a trembling voice, he said, "That corpsman was a friend of mine, and he's not doing too well."

I replied, "If it's any comfort to you, I tried to help him, but I was too far away."

He reached for my hand and said, "Thanks." Then he added, "Get over to the doc's office."

With no crutches, I hopped over to the office. "Corporal Kaquatosh, will you tell me what happened last night?" the doctor asked me.

"The corpsman dropped the lantern, and everything went dark," I said.

"Someone used a 45 on those Japanese," he said. They had found the casings.

"The corpsman did a good job on them," I smiled.

"The corpsman had a carbine, and it was never fired."

"Sir, if I told you the truth, I'd be court-martialed."

"There won't be any court-martial."

"You better give the corpsman a medal," I said.

"We intend to give him a letter of commendation."

"I'm glad. He was a good man."

"I've got good news for you. There's a plane leaving for the states, and I'm going to make sure you're on it," he smiled.

"That's the best news I've heard in my whole life," I replied. "How can I thank you?"

"By getting rid of that 45 before some other officer finds it."

Maybe this incident brought out the best in me. I had a hard time holding back the tears. I asked the doctor this question: "Sir, I have always said no white man will ever make me cry, so, tell me, why do I have rain on my face?"

"Because you are human, like the rest of us," he said with a grin.

I told him about the can of beer Bob and I had been going to share. He looked at me with a sympathetic expression and said, "There are times when we can only do so much for a person, and we lose him. We hate ourselves when we can't save him. Know what I mean?"

I told him, "Now I know what you meant about being human."

He said, "You're learning."

I smiled at that one.

"We better get you to the airport. They're holding a plane for you. On behalf of the US Navy, I thank you."

"Sir, it's me who owes thanks for getting my ankle well. I'll never forget how well you have treated me here. Thanks."

"Anything you want, just ask," he added.

"There's a can of beer buried under my bed. Will you take a few sips from it and pour the rest on the ground for Bob and the corpsman?"

"I'll take care of everything," he said with a smile, and he reached for my hand. I'll always remember that firm handshake.

"Your jeep just pulled up. Good luck to you."

I hopped onto the jeep and waved to him as the driver headed for the airstrip.

On the way to the airport, I could still smell the effluvia emanating from the corpses on that island. That foul-smelling vapor haunts me to this day.

41

Homeward Bound

The corpsman gave me a fast ride to the airstrip. As we approached the plane, a C-54 four-engine transport, it was warming up two of its engines. On the side of the plane was a ladder. I knew I'd have trouble climbing it because my ankle hurt with every step.

Standing by the door was a crew chief, and he was watching me limp toward the plane. I managed to climb up and enter the plane, and the chief said, "We don't take casualties on this plane."

Then the captain appeared and asked, "What's the holdup?"

The chief said, "We have a casualty here."

The captain looked at him and said, "Close the door!" The chief seemed confused. He wouldn't back off, so the captain said, "You are now on report for disobeying orders. You will remain on this ship when we reach Guam." He looked at me and said, "Corporal, when we get airborne, report to me in the cockpit."

"Yes, sir," I replied.

He said, "You must be someone special, or the chief surgeon wouldn't have asked me to hold the plane for you."

One of my friends had packed my seabag and put it with all the others aboard the plane. Just after takeoff, someone said, "Look Ray! Bloody Nose Ridge!" I peered out the window and gazed at the huge white cross marking the place where five hundred Marines had died. *How lucky can I get?* I thought.

After a while, the pilot sent for me. On the way to the cockpit, I was amazed at all the dials and gauges and lights, and that was just in the engineer's compartment. Then I saw the cockpit, with more gauges and dials. What an array of equipment! At that moment, I knew someday I'd be a pilot. After all, wasn't I Little Hawk?

When the captain noticed me, he said, "How about a ham sandwich and a glass of milk?"

He handed me a cup of milk and a real ham sandwich. I couldn't believe it. I said, "I haven't had a ham sandwich or milk in over a year and a half."

Then he said, "If we were stateside, I'd buy you the best dinner in the house."

I asked him, "Why the red carpet treatment?" He didn't answer, and I let it go at that.

When I had finished my sandwich, he turned to me and said, "The doctor who took care of you at the hospital is a good friend of mine. He told me the Navy owes you a favor." He smiled and asked, "Will you tell me more about what happened back there?"

"I broke naval regulations and might get court-martialed for it," I replied.

"Not if I can prevent it," he said with a smile.

"Two Japs tried to kill the corpsman. Someone blasted them with a 45 and sent them to join their ancestors. Because I was the only half-ambulatory patient in the whole ward, they blamed me for it," I answered. Then I told him, "The doc said he would never reveal anything. And here's another fact—someone buried a 45 under my bed."

He smiled and asked, "Who would do a crazy thing like that?"

"Only a crazy Indian," I said, laughing.

He burst out laughing and said, "I agree with the doctor."

We began to feel turbulence, and he said, "It's getting a little rough. You better get back to your seat and fasten your seatbelt." He told me to report back when the turbulence had subsided.

The plane would drop one hundred to two hundred feet at a time. Each time, I'd almost become weightless for a few seconds; then I was pushed down on my seat so hard it made my arms feel heavy. All the seabags and mailbags were tossed around as well.

With the plane's four Pratt & Whitney engines moaning and groaning, the pilot climbed higher to get above the storm. Finally he leveled off. The temperature had been over 100 degrees when we left Peleliu, but now it was cold, and I had to wrap a mailbag around myself. Our ears became blocked and we had to shout at each other.

After we got away from the storm, the pilot started to descend, and every time I swallowed, my ears made a cracking sound. Then the air got warmer, and I could hear better.

The captain sent for me and said, "The chief might give us a little grief, so when we land on Guam, I want you to stay aboard and keep him with you." Then he told me, "The chief was right. We can't transport casualties."

"How can I hold him on this ship?" I asked.

"I'll give you my 45. I'm sure you know how to use it," he laughed.

Once again I fastened my seatbelt, and the plane began to descend. I felt a jolt, and I knew we had touched down. We rolled along the runway until a jeep came alongside and passed us.

Everyone was happy and shaking hands with each other. Someone said, "Look at all the clean buildings!"

I looked out and didn't see any black smoke anywhere. When we were parked, the chief opened the door. We got a breath of clean air. What a relief. No stench from decaying bodies, and no snipers to worry about.

The jeep driver motioned the pilot to cut the two inner engines. The captain emerged from the cockpit and said, "Everyone except the crew chief and the corporal have permission to disembark from this ship."

Everyone else left the plane. Then the captain said to the chief, "This corporal will be responsible for you while I am gone. You will remain with this ship until we reach Johnston Island. Corporal, here's my 45. Put on the duty belt. Careful, it's loaded."

"That's the kind I like, and thank you, sir," I replied as I snapped to attention.

The captain looked at the chief and asked, "Why didn't you come to attention when speaking to an officer?"

The chief said, "I am sorry, sir. It won't happen again." He looked a little flushed.

The captain said, "At ease!" After he left, I turned to the chief and remarked, "That's a damn good officer."

The chief replied, "I could take that gun away from you and whip you."

"Try to stop me from going home, and I'll plug you too like I did last night to those two Japanese."

"How long have you been out here?" asked the chief.

"Since August '43," I replied.

He paused. "I believe you would shoot me," he said.

"Now you're making sense," I said.

"Don't worry. I won't give you any trouble. What happened to your leg?"

"Sniper got lucky, and it hurts with each step."

"You need anything, just ask," said the chief.

"There is one thing. Apologize to the captain."

"Sure, I'll do it as soon as he comes back," the chief replied.

"Wait until after takeoff."

The captain sent us a dinner fit for a king, and we ate it as the other men began getting back on the plane. When the captain returned, he walked over to us and asked, "Is everything all right?"

The chief said, "Yes, sir. Is there anything I can do for you, sir?"

The captain handed him his briefcase and told him to take it forward, then turned to me and asked, "What happened to the chief?"

I told him that we had a little talk and that once we were airborne, we would like to have a moment of his time. The captain said he'd send for us.

Soon we were flying again. It was a clear day, and we ascended higher and higher until I could see small clouds far below us. Nothing but blue above. It was so still you could write a letter and not mess it up. I thought of my wolf and my little sister. I wondered how they were and how things were at home. The chief jolted me back to reality when he jerked my arm and said, "The captain wants to talk to us."

When I tried to walk, my ankle gave me a sharp pain and I

almost fell forward. The chief caught my arm and said, "Need a little help?"

I told him, "I need a crutch."

"You got one."

He helped me to the radio compartment. The captain said, "You wanted to see me?"

"Sir, I'd like to apologize for disobeying your orders," the chief said.

"Okay, chief. See that it doesn't happen again."

"Yes, sir. Are there any further orders?" replied the chief.

"Keep an eye on the starboard engines."

"Yes, sir, and thank you," the chief said as he exited the cockpit.

"Corporal, what did you tell the chief?" the pilot asked me.

"To be a little more considerate of others, and that it's better to have friends than enemies. Someday he'll need a friend," I said.

"He seems like a new man," the captain said.

"He's a good man, and I hope you don't court-martial him," I said. I hobbled back to my seat, strapped on my seatbelt, and fell asleep.

After a while, the chief pulled on my arm again and told me the captain would be making an announcement. The captain opened the door and said, "When we land on Johnston Island, I'll be leaving you. A new crew will fly you to Pearl Harbor. It's been a pleasure to help you men back. Good luck."

After another smooth landing, a jeep guided us to a parking spot. Everyone got off the plane, and the chief waited for the captain to approach. "Sir, I'd like permission to stay aboard until the new crew chief gets here, so I can square him away," the chief said.

"Permission granted." He turned to me, extended his hand, and said, "Corporal, I leave you in good hands. It's been a pleasure meeting you."

We shook hands. I said, "Captain, the next time you see the doctor on Peleliu, tell him I'll never forget what the Navy did for me. Thanks again."

The Navy and the Marines do not salute indoors or when they don't have a cap on, and officers don't salute enlisted men. But as the captain was leaving, he turned quickly and saluted me. Before I could snap to attention, he was out the door. That was the only time an officer ever saluted me.

"Well, I'll be damned," the chief said. Then he asked me, "What would you like from the mess hall?"

"Steak," I answered.

About a half an hour later, he handed me my steak. I couldn't wait. "Where did you get this?" I asked.

He smiled and said, "Some chief petty officer will be out of a dinner tonight. Those chiefs eat too much."

It was my first steak in about fourteen months, and I enjoyed every bite.

The new crew chief stepped aboard while I was eating and asked, "Why isn't he eating in the mess hall?"

The old chief took him aside. They talked for a while and came back. The new chief said, "I'd like to shake your hand. Anything you need from now on, just ask." The old chief just smiled. We waved until he was out of sight.

The flight from Johnston Island to Pearl Harbor was not as tiresome as the flight from Peleliu. It seemed like we had just gotten settled and we were landing.

Everyone started to move out of the plane. The new crew chief came over and said, "Better wait until the pilots leave, and I'll help you get down the ladder." (These pilots didn't know I was a casualty.) When I got on the ground, the chief threw my seabag over his shoulder. I held on to his belt, and we walked to the terminal.

The chief said, "We made it." With a sigh of relief, I sat on a bench. He reached down and shook my hand. I thanked him, and he said, "No sweat."

He left and a little later came back with a wheelchair. "Where did you get that?" I asked.

"I borrowed it from the Army." He wheeled me over to sick bay and said, "I better get this back before they know it's missing." He waved to me as he left the building.

After a year and a half of dehydrated potatoes, eggs, milk, and chlorinated water and two months of stench-filled air, I was back in civilization.

42

Naval Hospital

It was December 1944, a little over three years since the Japanese had bombed Pearl Harbor. Now the place looked peaceful as we passed over all the ships that lay on the bottom of the harbor. One battleship, the *Arizona,* could be seen with its mast still flying the flag. Hickam Field seemed completely repaired when we landed. All they had to do now was fix my ankle.

I intended to get bombed before they tried to put me back in a cast, but it didn't work out that way. They took me straight to sick bay from the terminal. There I was given crutches to hobble around on. I couldn't help thinking how lucky I was to be back here. Everything seemed sparkling clean. Even the sheets were nice and clean.

I hated to sit on the bed in my dirty dungarees. There was still some dried blood on my pants leg bottom, and my shoe was split down the side to allow room for the swelling. A corpsman handed me a bundle of clothes, along with a robe and a razor, toothbrush, and a bar of soap with towels. He said, "Put all your clothes in that bag, and I'll send them to the laundry."

While taking my clothes out of my seabag, I found a duty belt with a 45 holster and two clips of ammo. I quickly rolled all of them up and hid them back in my seabag. After I took a shower, I wanted to get a little shuteye, so I rested on the clean bed and closed my eyes, thinking of my wolf back on the reservation. I knew it was cold back there, but my wolf was right in his element. He always seemed to enjoy winter more than the hot summers. Someday we would be together again.

Sometime later, I was awakened by a nurse. "Wake up, corporal," she said. "And how are we today?"

"I don't know about you, but I'm sleepy."

"Open your mouth. That's a good boy."

"Twenty years old, been shot at and missed, shot at and hit, and I'm not a boy," I said.

"What happened to your ankle?"

"Sniper got lucky."

"How long were you over there?"

"About a year and a half."

"You must have been lonesome."

"No, I had my wolf's picture with me."

"Are you on medication?" she asked.

"Yes, I have pills for malaria."

"I hope you like it here in Pearl Harbor," she said.

"I'm looking forward to exploring the island to check out some of those hula skirts," I replied.

"Be careful," she warned.

"Tell that to the hula skirts!"

She left me alone for a while. That nurse must have been twenty-five years old, too old for me. Besides, she was an officer. What I needed was a twenty-year-old in a hula skirt. Then I looked at my foot and remembered I wasn't going anywhere.

The nurse was back. "Corporal, I'm taking you down to X-ray." She gestured to a wheelchair.

At X-ray she told me, "Step in that room and take your clothes off."

"Why do I have to take my clothes off to X-ray my ankle?"

"Chest X-ray."

"There's nothing wrong with my chest—it's my ankle!"

"Doctor's orders."

So there I sat, naked, until a corpsman came in and said, "Put your clothes on!"

"Why?"

"I want to take a chest X-ray."

See how those hospitals worked? One told you to take your clothes off, the other told you to put them on. What next?

"You can leave now, we're done," the corpsman told me.

"I can't. The nurse took my crutches." I moaned and limped toward the ward.

Here came my nurse again. "Why are you walking on that ankle?" she asked.

"You took my crutches."

"Get in the chair!

Next the men in white coats came to see me. One pointed at my ankle. The other looked at my chart, shook his head, and said, "Hmmm . . ."

After they talked for a long time, one of them said, "Corporal, we're sending you over to a specialist." I hobbled down the corridor, walked for a half mile, and finally asked someone where to find a bone specialist.

"That way, to the next right, go four doors, turn left, all the way down the hall until you come to the first exit, then turn right at the main entrance, then go right until you see the nurses' desk, turn right, and go about two doors down on the left. You can't miss it."

After walking for another half hour, I sat down to rest. A nurse came along and asked, "Are you looking for the orthopedic department?"

"Do they fix bones there?" After she answered yes, I asked, "How many miles is it from here?"

She pointed to a door and said, "It's right there."

"Thank you. I was about to call a cab."

———

After I was admitted to the naval hospital, I had nothing to do but wait. It seemed every time I fell asleep, I was awakened for some test, and most often it was just to take my temperature. My ankle was really paining me, and the pills they gave me didn't seem to help.

With so much time on my hands, my mind began to wander, and my imagination became active. Once when the nurse appeared I asked, "Can I have my crutches?"

"You won't be needing them," she said.

Uh-oh, now I knew I'd had it.

With all those negative thoughts, I felt like a candidate for the loony bin—that is, if I wasn't already in it. *Maybe I could go over the north wall when the moon comes out,* I thought. After the nurse checked me out, she said, "I'll be back at 2400 [midnight]."

Come midnight, here came my nurse. "Corporal, you are not to eat or drink anything until after your next X-rays." She smiled and walked away. I thought, *By the time I get my X-rays, I'll be dead from malnutrition and dehydration.*

Early the next morning, more men in white coats approached my bed. They didn't even look at my ankle. One took my chart from the end of my bed, and the other two looked at it over his shoulder. I thought, *If I tell them my head is bothering me, maybe they'll check my ankle.*

One asked, "Are you experiencing any pain?"

"Only when they take my blood and when I walk."

"We'll get that ankle checked in X-ray soon."

Along came my nurse again. "Corporal, I'm sending you down to the X-ray department."

"You're not taking me?"

"The corpsman will take you."

"Does he have a driver's license?" The corpsman motioned to me to get in the wheelchair and started speeding me toward the X-ray department.

"Go in that room and take your pants off!" he ordered.

"You gonna X-ray my head?" I joked.

"Slow down!" I screamed as the corpsman hurried me back to the ward. Too late. He drove me against the wall to avoid a collision with a man on a gurney.

"Are you hurt?"

"I don't know, I'm in shock. I wanna go back to Peleliu."

Back in the ward, the nurse asked me, "How was your trip to the X-ray department?"

"They should have given the corpsman a ticket for speeding. He drove me into a wall!"

"Are you hurt?"

"Ask my lawyer!"

Finally the ward doctor informed me: "Corporal, all you need is plenty of rest. Stay off your ankle as much as possible, and you'll be discharged in a few days."

How lucky could I get?

43

Angel in Wausau

Late in December 1944 I left Pearl Harbor on a transport ship. It seemed like only a day or two had passed when someone hollered, "Land ho!" and I saw the prettiest sight I'd seen in more than a year: the mainland of the good old USA. Soon we were entering the port of San Francisco. A small boat approached the portside of the ship, and we took on a pilot. He knew where all the mines were planted, and he guided us into port.

One of the men said, "Look, Ray, the Golden Gate Bridge!" I turned and took a long look at that lovely sight. I had made it. I was back in the states after seventeen months in the South Pacific.

When we were going under the bridge, I thought the ship's mast was going to hit it, but we passed right under. The tugboats pushed the ship against the dock, and the gangplanks came down. We poured out like bats out of hell. One guy got down and kissed the pavement. We were hollering and dancing around with our arms waving. My ankle even felt better.

Buses were waiting to take us to Mare Island Naval Base, each with a woman driver. From Mare Island we were driven over the Golden Gate Bridge and on to El Toro Marine Corps Base in Santa Ana. There we were issued new uniforms and shoes.

A couple weeks later, just after New Year's Day 1945, we were given thirty days' furlough. With new clothes and new suitcases for our belongings, we headed for the buses that would take us to the Los Angeles train station. There we boarded the streamlined train *El Capitan,* bound for Chicago.

Riding in first class was a pleasure. We had our own beds, reclining seats, and the use of a club car and dining car. It took about four days to get to Chicago, and I enjoyed every part of the trip.

From Chicago I took the North Shore train to Milwaukee, and from there I boarded a bus to Wausau. I was just placing my suitcase in the rack above the seats when I heard someone holler, "Corporal!" I looked toward the back of the bus and was surprised to see another man in a Marine uniform. He was also a corporal. He told me his name was Jim Henderson and he was from Antigo, Wisconsin.

I asked, "What outfit are you in?"

"First Division," he answered. That's the Marine Corps division that made history on Guadalcanal. He told me had joined the Marines before the Japanese bombed Pearl Harbor, and he had been there and at all the other battles the First Division endured, all the way to Peleliu. Then we had to talk about Bloody Nose Ridge and those stinking bodies and the huge flies.

Jim was the most decorated Marine I had ever had the pleasure of meeting. He didn't mention how he got the Silver Star or any of his other medals. He never bragged or talked about the war or how many men he had killed. Partly this was because we were having such a good time catching up on all the things we had missed while in the Marines. With him was his future wife, Ginny, who lived in Wausau.

Jim needed a place to stay while he visited Ginny, so we decided to share a room at the Wausau Hotel. We took a cab to Charlie Armond's bar, near Rib Mountain. We liked the tavern's large dance floor and the view of Lake Wausau. We decided we'd return soon, but for now we needed some shuteye, so we went to get our hotel keys. A redhead handed me mine. She had greenish eyes and wore her hair piled on top of her head.

On the way to our room, I almost cold-cocked myself by walking into the elevator door. Who cares? I had just met an angel, and her name was Maye. Jim asked me a question, but I didn't answer.

"Did you see her?" I sighed.

"See who?" Jim asked.

"The redhead at the desk," I told him.

After I described her, he said, "You've been drinking too much. When you drink too much, all women look like movie stars."

"I'll never look at another woman," I said.

"Calm down. I'll go check her out. She can't be that beautiful," Jim replied.

When Jim didn't return, I went to find him in the bar. Sitting in a booth with a glass of beer in his hand, he looked a little worried. He looked up at me and said, "Ray, you're not drunk. She is beautiful."

A little while later, Maye walked in. "Is everything all right?" she asked.

"It would be a lot nicer if you joined us," I told her.

"I'd love to, but I'm on duty until seven a.m.," she said.

"I'm gonna sit by your desk until seven a.m.," I said.

She smiled. "No need to. I'll call you."

I turned to Jim and asked, "Did you hear that?" He just smiled and took a long drink.

When we got back to our room, I called Maye and asked her to give me a call at 6:30 so I could get dressed for breakfast. "I hope your boyfriend won't mind," I said.

She quickly replied, "I don't have a boyfriend." At that, I dropped the phone and rushed to get my clothes back on.

When I got back downstairs, some drunk was giving Maye a hard time. She pushed him away. "Need some help?" I asked.

The guy looked at me and said, "Oh, we have a big, brave man here!"

"I'm not big and brave, but if I catch you messing around with my angel, you'll be picking your teeth up off the floor."

He quickly backed off and said, "Oh, I didn't know she had a Marine boyfriend."

Maye rushed around the desk, threw her arms around my neck, and kissed my cheek. "You missed my lips by that much," I smiled. She didn't miss the second time. Her lipstick was still on my lips when her boss walked in.

"This is Ray, my boyfriend," Maye quickly told her boss.

"She's been talking about you for a long time," her boss said. She smiled and said, "Why don't you two go out and have a cup of coffee? There's a shop open on the corner."

It was ten degrees below zero as we walked to the coffee shop, but I was as warm as toast. It could be raining, snowing, hailing for all I cared. You couldn't have given me a finer night.

As we sat down in a booth, Maye seemed eager to tell me something. "Ray, I owe you an explanation," she began. "My old boyfriend was named Ray. He just got married."

"Remind me to thank him," I said.

"Why did you call me your angel?"

"You are my angel. You just don't have wings," I told her.

The next morning, I answered Maye's call at 6:30 and was soon standing in front of her desk with my dress blue uniform on. She didn't see me until she turned and dropped the letters she was holding.

"That's the prettiest uniform I've ever seen!" she said.

"We use them only on special occasions, and this is the most important moment in my life."

She gave me a smile and said, "Mine too."

We had the longest breakfast in the history of the Wausau Cafe. I don't recall what we ate, but who cares?

That night we had plans to go to dinner and a movie after Maye got off work. Things were going too smoothly. I'd better watch out.

44

Bar Room Brawl

After Maye went to work at the hotel that night, Jim and I decided to go to a tavern. The cab driver said the Terrace Gardens was a nice place. It turned out to be the same bar owned by Charlie Armond that we had visited earlier.

The bar was so packed we couldn't get a stool. But we were used to standing in line.

Before we even had a chance to take a drink, a soldier from Camp McCoy* hollered, "Hey, we got two heroes here!"

Then Jim took off his coat, and everyone could see the ribbons on his shirt. The comments behind us quieted down for a moment. Jim wore the Silver Star, the Purple Heart, the pre–Pearl Harbor Medal, and a few others. I had only two decks of ribbons and one battle star. I felt like a Boy Scout next to him.

As we settled in for some serious drinking, I could still hear unkind remarks coming from the crowd. "Just ignore them," Jim said.

"Bullshit! If those guys want to know what the Marines are made of, they're barking up the right tree," I said.

---

* Camp McCoy (now called Fort McCoy) is a US Army training facility near Tomah, Wisconsin. During World War II the post was also used as a prisoner-of-war camp.

Jim looked at me. "That's what I like about you Indians. You're always looking for a good fight."

I told him my ankle still hurt and asked how bad his wound was. "All healed up," he said. "Hope you can back me up if I get my ass kicked," I told him.

"You won't get your ass kicked while I'm around," he smiled.

"That's what I like about you shock troops.* Always looking for a good fight!" We laughed and clinked glasses.

We didn't have to wait long. A guy came over and said, "Is it true you bought all those ribbons at a dime store?"

Jim looked at me and said, "How 'bout that?"

I turned to face the man and asked, "Are you talking to me or him?"

"I don't care who I'm talking to," the man said.

"Would you care to have the next dance?" I asked.

"Why you son of a . . . " He drew back his fist, but before he could deliver it, I clipped him with a left to the nose. He fell backwards and hit his head on the bar foot rail. He seemed a little dazed, so I reached down and helped him up.

"Who hit me?" he asked.

"The guy behind you." I pointed to a man with his back toward us. He spun the guy around and hit him with a hard right and a left; they both fell to the floor. They struggled back to their feet and started to swing at each other. One accidentally hit the soldier who was standing next to me, knocking him toward the bar.

Then that guy started coming at us, and Jim yelled, "Hold my beer!"

---

* "Shock troops" is a nickname for military units trained to lead surprise attacks.

With a beer in each hand, I tried to stay clear of the melee. The soldier hit Jim and was rewarded with a straight right to the face. He flew against the wall. Someone else jumped on Jim's back and was flipped forward. Then another one came at Jim from the side but quickly received a chop on the neck and was down for the count.

"Aren't you going to dance?" Jim asked me.

"Nobody will hold our beers," I replied.

"Look out for that guy behind you," Jim warned. Too late. Someone pushed me, and I dumped our beers all over the floor. Now, that's grounds for a court-martial. No man is going to spill my beer and get away with it.

Suddenly we heard a BANG! Charlie must have saved some firecrackers and had thrown one into the midst of the fight. Everyone stopped.

Charlie yelled, "Did you guys come here to drink, or fight?"

I was about to yell back, but Jim said, "We need six beers."

"That's more like it," Charlie said.

Finally we could drink our beers. Soon I thought I was getting drunk, and I told Jim I wasn't feeling too good. "Better knock off the beer," he told me. Then I started shivering and sweating.

"You look pale," Jim said.

"Malaria," I said. We both knew what that meant. The soldiers flocked around us and wanted to know if they could help. Jim told them to call a cab.

"We gotta get him to sick bay . . . fast!"

When we got in the cab, I asked the driver to turn down the heat. "It's fifteen below zero," he said. Jim told the driver I was having a malaria attack, but he didn't understand. My arms were getting a little heavy and my head hurt. Then I began to get sleepy.

Jim helped me up the steps of the hotel and into our room. Then he called Maye. She rushed into our room and wanted to know what was wrong. Jim told her, "Call a doctor, quickly!" She got on the phone and told the manager to call a doctor and send him to our room.

I was freezing and shaking. Jim put my overcoat on me, and Maye got another blanket. She sat at my bedside and looked worried. I took her hand and tried to assure her that I'd be all right. "I'm not leaving you," she said.

Jim said, "I've got some pills for malaria." I told him I couldn't take them after I drank more than four bottles of beer. "You're right," he said.

The doctor arrived. He took one look at me and said, "We better get him to the hospital." He asked if I was on any medication.

"Just five bottles of beer to kill the pain."

"What pain?" he asked.

"My ankle was broken, and it flares up once in a while."

"We're taking you to the hospital, now."

Maye rushed to get her coat as Jim helped me back into a cab.

45

St. Mary's Hospital

All night long and part of the next morning, Maye stayed by my side at the hospital. When I woke, she asked, "Ray, do you have a wolf?"

"Am I in the loony bin?" I answered.

"You've been delirious most of the night and morning," she said. She told me that I still had a high fever and the doctors were thinking of packing me in ice.

My temperature started to get back to normal the next day. Maye visited me every day for about a week. The temperature outside remained below zero, and I was concerned about her health. I told her not to come out when it was so cold. She just smiled and said, "Okay. I'll see you soon."

During my first week at St. Mary's, a priest began to visit me. I learned later he had cancer, but he never told me. He never complained and seemed more concerned about my health. He prayed over my bedside all night long. One night I had a nightmare and started to holler and shake. I dreamed some Japs were going to bayonet me, and I was reaching under my pillow for my 45 but couldn't find it. The priest turned the lights on and calmed me down. How foolish I felt.

The nightmares continued. One day I told a nun about them. I told her I was trying to forget those bloody events on Peleliu. The nun said, "You must be thinking about those horrible times while you're awake." She was right. I couldn't forget what I had done.

"I suppose I'll go straight to hell for what I did."

She looked at me with sympathetic eyes. She said, "I would have done the same thing you did, and I wouldn't give a hoot about those guys after what they did to the others."

Then I asked, "Do you think I'll be condemned for what I did?"

She quickly told me, "Of course not!" That night I had a really good sleep, and I felt better from that day on.

Now all I wanted was to get out of there. But how could I leave when I couldn't even stand up? I'd just have to wait it out. The nurses told me that it was Saturday. No wonder I was weak. I'd had nothing to eat since Tuesday, but I wasn't even hungry.

One day while Maye was visiting me, the nun came in and said, "The Good Father wants to know if he can come in."

"Tell him to come right in," I replied.

"Ray, I'm going to leave you now," the priest said. "Take these prayer beads and my book, and promise me you'll read it from time to time."

"Father, why didn't you tell me you were sick? I asked.

"Because it's hopeless," he said. "I prayed for you all night, and I hope you will go back to church. Will you?'"

"I'll be in the chapel as soon as I can walk, and I'll always keep your beads, and I'll read the whole book," I promised.

The nurse came in and said, "Father, we're taking you down to emergency."

"It's too late, and I want to finish talking to Ray."

"Father, you better go down to emergency," I told him.

"I want you to do one more thing for me."

"Name it!" I said.

"Forget about those dreams, and trust in God," he said.

"I'll do that. I want you to know I really appreciate what you have done for me. I'll never forget it," I told him.

They wheeled him out, and he never came back.

I can still see him sitting there and asking me to go back to church and to trust in God. I lived up to my promise, and someday we shall meet again. It's only a matter of time.

I walked slowly back to my bed. I covered my eyes and asked Maye to pull the shades. I could feel the emotion building up and tears forming. I couldn't face Maye, so I turned my head toward the window. She held my hand and squeezed.

I said to her, "When I was on grave detail on the island of Pele-liu, I had to bury many men. Some were teenagers. We wrapped them in blankets and covered them in the sand. On all these occasions, I never cried. I have always said that no white man will ever make me cry. Maye, I'm a full-blooded Indian, and men in our family do not cry."

She placed her head against mine and sat motionless for a few moments. I could feel her sobbing. I asked her, "Tell me, why are these tears in my eyes? Am I getting weak like the whites? My friend Bob didn't make it. I cried then. Now I lost the Good Father, and I'm crying again. I can't take this any longer. Please call the nurse."

Two nurses rushed in and asked what was wrong. I said, "I just lost another friend and I can't take it anymore. Please give me something to ease the pain." One of them, slender and elegant with jet-black hair, put her hand on my forehead. She said, "His fever is coming back." The other nurse returned with a hypodermic syringe and injected something into my arm. I began to slowly drift off.

Sometime later, I smelled the sweet scent of violets. I opened my eyes, and the dark-haired nurse was adjusting my pillow. She smiled and said, "My name is Delores. I'll be your night nurse again."

"You must be new here," I said.

"No, I've been watching over you since you got here."

"Today is the first day I've eaten since Tuesday," I told her.

"I know. You had me worried for a while," she replied.

"I'm getting hungry," I said.

"Good. Supper will be ready in a little while." She left and soon returned with a tray of food. "Tell me about yourself," she said.

"I'm a Menominee Indian from Neopit. Joined the Marines when I was seventeen, shipped overseas in 1943, and returned this January. I turned twenty last July."

"Do you have a wolf?" she asked. Like Maye, she must have heard me talking about the wolf while I was feverish.

"Yes, his name is Kernel."

"When was the last time you saw him?" she asked.

"January 1942," I replied.

"You haven't seen him since you got back?" she seemed surprised.

"No," I said. "I got sick the second night here in Wausau."

"I'd like to see him," she remarked.

"He'd like you."

"Why?" she asked.

"He likes all women, just like me—even though we're both lone wolves," I said.

"You're kidding me," she laughed.

"No, it's a fact. Wolves are hard to tame, but affectionate," I told her.

———

Soon I was feeling stronger and I could get in and out of bed. I had to thank the Great Spirit for being kind to me. Most important, I needed to make a trip to the chapel and pray for the Good Father.

The next time a nurse came in, I asked her if I could get in uniform and go down to the chapel. "I don't see why not," she said.

After I got dressed, I waited for Maye. When she arrived, she took a quick look at me and said, "You're in uniform."

"I promised the Good Father I'd go to church," I said.

Christians have prayers to say while in church. Instead of prayers, some Indians talk with their Creator like he is standing in their presence. I told my Creator that I would take care of the father's beads and his book and I would read it from time to time. Also, I asked him to tell the father I would see him someday in the Happy Hunting Ground. And I thanked him for letting me live another day.

On the way back to my room, I suddenly felt sick again. The nurses helped me to my bed, and I fell into a deep sleep.

Later the doctor woke me. I saw that it was dark outside, and the nurses were standing alongside my bed. "Who gave you permission to get out of bed?" the doctor asked.

"No one. I felt so good today. I stole my uniform from the closet and made good on my promise."

"What promise?" he asked.

"The one I made to the Good Father before he left for the Happy Hunting Ground," I told him.

"You better stay in bed until your temperature gets back to normal," he stated. "Malarial fever takes a long time to go into remission, and sometimes it comes back unexpectedly." Before he left, he turned and gave me this last piece of advice: "Don't get out of bed until your temperature is lower than 100 degrees."

The nurse whom I had asked for permission to get out of bed was standing near me. She reached to adjust my pillow and whispered, "Thanks for not giving me away."

"Oh, I'd never give you away. I need you to adjust my pillow and give me my pills."

"Maye, is he always this nice to people?" the nurse asked.

"He's an angel sometimes," Maye replied.

"Hey, I'm the only one who can use that name," I said.

"See what I mean?" Maye asked.

"I'll close the door so you two can be alone," the nurse said.

"Now, young man, you didn't tell me about your fever," Maye turned to me and glared.

"It goes up every time I hold your hand."

"Will you be serious?" Maye asked.

"Sure. I want to make mad passionate love to you as soon as I get out of here," I warned her.

"I can't wait," she smiled.

"We better not. The nuns have large books here," I said.

"What's this about nuns and large books?" she asked.

"When I was in the orphanage, a nun hit me with a book," I explained.

"You didn't tell me about being in an orphanage," she said.

"I know. I didn't want to make you cry."

"I promise not to cry. I want to know all about you," she said.

"For now, why don't you tell me about yourself?"

"Well, I got out of high school last spring and got my first job. I got engaged, he married someone else, and then I met you. I'm nineteen and in love with you and I hope you love me, too."

"You better call that nurse back," I told her. "I think I'm dreaming or delirious. You're the first person I've met who really seems to mean what they say. I have a lot of love stored up. You're the one person who has shown any compassion for me. Now, call the nurse so they can take me to the loony bin!"

"You just made me the happiest person in the world!" Maye replied. "What's the loony bin?"

"That's the place where people wear pajamas with no backs and scream at you."

"Promise me you'll never change," she laughed.

46

Premonition

In my second week at St. Mary's, I was permitted to walk around, and I felt stronger. One morning when Maye came to visit, I surprised her in the corridor. "Any angels out today?" I asked from behind her.

She turned and said, "Only for my Raymond." Then she threw her arms around my neck and gave me a kiss.

"Wow! You pack a better punch than the Irishman I fought back at the Marine base."

She surprised me by replying, "Well, I'm Irish."

I thought for a moment and said, "Irishmen and Indians are the most stubborn, proud, and boastful people on earth, and they never give up."

She smiled, took my hand, and said, "Ray, you're right."

"Good news," I smiled too. I told her my temperature was back to normal and that I could go out during the day, but I had to be back by suppertime. "Tomorrow I can go to a movie if you want to."

We spent the rest of morning in the sunroom talking about trivial things. Then she asked about my wolf.

"He's about ten years old," I told her.

"Is he mean?" she asked.

"Only when he's provoked. Then, look out!" I said.

"That scares me," she replied.

"He's gentle as a lamb, but he's killed two dogs."

"Why?" she asked.

"They both attacked me and wouldn't back off."

"Did he ever bite you?" she wondered.

"Never! But you have to let him know who's boss," I told her.

She wasn't thrilled about my wolf, and I wasn't thrilled about her reaction. I felt the inkling of a premonition. Now that I had found out Maye was suspicious of my wolf, I became suspicious of her.

Still, on my first liberty to leave the hospital, I was eager to surprise Maye. She had been waiting for this moment all week. My dress blue uniform was still in the closet in my room. I put it on and went to wait for Maye.

The hospital gift shop was located next to the main entrance. I waited there by the door and made sure she didn't see me when she entered. As she passed me, I walked behind her and said again, "Any angels out today?" She turned and gave me a long kiss. As we stood there, people had to walk around us, and they all just smiled; even a few nuns smiled as they passed.

We headed out to catch the bus. It was still below zero, but it didn't matter if it was hot or cold, all I could think of was how lucky I was. On our way downtown, Maye told me, "Jim called and said he'd be at the hotel this afternoon. You'd better stop and see if he's there."

Our first stop was the Mint Café for lunch. Maye asked what it had been like overseas, and I told her the islands were beautiful but the water and food were terrible. Then she asked about the war. "Not while I'm eating," I said.

"That bad?" she asked.

I told her, "Don't ever ask Jim or me how many men we killed." Maye looked at me with sympathetic eyes and said, "I'm sorry."

When we were finished eating, the café owner came to our table and told us our meal was on him. He said his wife worked at the hospital, and she had told him about a patient who was a Marine. He knew it had to be me. "Good luck to you both," he said as we left the café.

As we walked to the hotel, the snow cracked with every step and steam poured out of our noses with every breath, but I never felt cold. Once there, Maye went to check in with her boss, and I peeked in the bar room. There sat Jim with his back to me.

I walked over and asked, "Any Marines from the 1st Divee?"

He turned and shouted, "Ray, you old son of a . . ."

I interrupted and said, "Watch your language! There's civilians around." Then I asked, "How was your trip to Antigo?"

"Great! I'm getting married," he said.

"They have a room up in the hospital for you—in the loony bin!" I laughed.

"Wanna be my best man?" he asked.

"Weddings and funerals I stay away from. One, you lose part of your freedom; the other, you lose it all," I replied.

———

Later, back at the hospital, I lay on my bed and thought of all the nice things Maye had done for me and how she had stayed by my side all the time I was sick. It seemed I had just closed my eyes when someone said, "Ray, I have to take your temperature." I could smell the fragrance of violets. I knew it was the dark-haired nurse, Delores.

Delores told me that Maye had left me a message. She would not be able to keep our breakfast date. Her mother had gotten sick, and she had to go out of town after work. With a disappointed look, I turned to Delores and said, "Just when I can go down to the cafeteria, I have to eat alone."

She laughed and said, "We are not supposed to fraternize with patients, but if you happen to sit at a table, there's no reason why I can't join you."

As I went through the line for breakfast the next morning, I saw Delores sitting at a table in a quiet corner. With my tray in hand, I pretended to look for a place to sit. She saw me and waved. "Need a little company?" I asked.

"It's reserved for a corporal in the Marines," she laughed.

"We Indians don't need reservations," I said. That made her laugh again.

Over breakfast I told Delores that I would most likely be shipped overseas again.

"Are you going to ask Maye to wait for you?" she asked.

"No. I couldn't ask any woman to go through that agony," I stated.

"Is she aware of that?" she asked.

"No. If she waits for me, that will prove she's worth waiting for," I replied.

"Don't you trust her?" she asked.

"Let me put it this way. I've seen too many men crack up when they got their Dear John letter."

"Do you think Maye is going to do that to you?" she asked.

"I have a feeling, a premonition about it," I replied.

Soon Delores had to leave for a class. As she turned to go, she said, "By the way, wolves are not hard to tame. Just be nice to them, consistent, and rewarding."

"How did you know that?" I asked, surprised.

"I took a course in zoology," she said with a smile.

After we said goodbye, I glanced down at my plate. I realized I hadn't taken one bite of my eggs. What the hell was wrong with me? Loony bin, here I come!

47

Wolf Reunion

When I joined the Marines, my mother told me I must make an offering to the Great Spirit to watch over me. Now it was time to return home to the reservation and have a talk with my Creator to give thanks for my safe return from the war.

I wondered if my wolf would recognize me after all this time.

The bus stopped in Shawano. From there I had to hitchhike to Neopit. A driver picked me up within twenty minutes. He said he was returning to Shawano later that day, and I asked him if he'd give me a ride back. "Sure, I'll wait for you," he replied.

Thinking of my wolf gave me a feeling of ecstasy. But my rapture came to an abrupt stop when I stepped from the car and came face to face with an eighty-pound timber wolf.

He didn't remember me. The fur on his back stood up, and he showed his fangs. He growled and then circled me, still growling. No strangers dared to invade his territory. He stopped. I stopped.

"Kernel, don't you remember me?" I said. He turned his head, trying to figure out who I was. "Kernel, it's me!" I clapped my hands. That was his command to jump up on my arm. He wagged his tail, just a little. Then I said the magic words, "Wanna go huntin'?" That did it.

Now he jumped up on my arm with such force he knocked me over, and we rolled in the snow. He tugged at my arm, trying to help me up. Then my mother opened the door and shouted, "Kernel!" He ran to her, and I got up looking like Frosty the Snowman. I couldn't stop laughing.

My mother greeted me with a smile and a hug. "We got the telegram informing us you were wounded. How bad?" she asked.

"Just a nick on the ankle," I assured her. My little sister was standing behind my mother, and she smiled, stepped forward, and with tears in her eyes told me she was about to move to Milwaukee. She seemed more serious than I remembered.

When she told me about her reason for moving, I was shocked. My brothers had deserted from the Army and were at home, living off the allotment the government was sending my mother, which was intended for my sister. Apparently my brothers had a good time getting drunk every time my mother received a check.

That bad news was giving me a headache. Then I thought about my pills. I had to take one. Then came more bad news. My mother had married some guy who was a lumberjack, and he quit work when he knew she was getting an allotment check each month. I was fit to be tied.

I took Catherine aside and told her to write to me when she got a new address in Milwaukee. Then I asked her if she had any money. Our sister in Milwaukee had sent her a train ticket to get there, and that's all she had. I gave her fifty dollars. She was so happy that she started crying again. "Don't tell anyone!" I told her. My mother came in and asked why Catherine was crying. I said, "She hates to see me go."

When it was time for me to leave, Catherine surprised me with a kiss goodbye. We never displayed much affection.

Kernel was waiting outside when my ride arrived. He walked with me to the car, and I bent down and put my arm around his neck and said, "I'll be back, and we can go hunting and fishing again." I reached for his paw, and he lifted one up. We shook, and I closed the car door.

"That's quite an animal," the driver said.

"Pure wolf," I replied.

———

When I got on the bus in Shawano, I asked the driver if I could use the back seat, as I had just taken a pill for malarial fever and it was making me sleepy. I closed my eyes, and the next thing I knew, he was announcing, "We're in Wausau." The cab driver stopped in front of the main entrance at the hospital and asked, "Need any help getting up the steps?"

"No, I'll make it. I'm just a little weak." By the time I got to the elevator, I was about to collapse. I made it to my room, took off my overcoat, and threw it on the chair. I crawled on to the bed and fell asleep.

As the days passed, I kept feeling better and stronger, and finally the day came when I had to return to the Marine Corps base in California. I stopped at the nurses' desk on my way out. "I want to thank all of you for taking good care of me while I was sick. I'll always remember how kind you were to me. Thank you." I shook their hands, saving Delores for last. She reached out her hand, and I grasped it with both of mine. "I'll never forget the times you put those cold compresses on my forehead." She smiled and walked me to the elevator.

At the elevator doors, I took Delores in my arms and kissed her goodbye. What she said next surprised me. "What about Maye?"

"I told her I'd be leaving on the early morning bus, so I won't be seeing her until my next furlough. Any more questions?" She shook her head.

As I walked to the bus stop, I looked back to the hospital and saw Delores waving from a third-floor window. The bus driver opened the door. I waved one more time and stepped onto the bus.

On the long, lonely trip back to the base, I thought a lot about my situation, and I made quite a few trips to the club car. I couldn't believe that two women could love me. I still had doubts about Maye's feelings. Maybe I should have asked Delores to wait for me. But I couldn't ask any woman to do that. I was a Marine.

48

The Great Spirit Beckons Again

When I got off the train in Los Angeles, it was about seventy degrees. What a change from ten below zero. I jumped on the next bus to Santa Ana and settled back. I was home for the time being.

After I got settled in the new barracks, I looked for some of my old buddies but found none of them. Next, I checked the mailroom, and to my surprise, I had two letters—one from Maye and one from Delores. Not bad for a lil' ol' corporal. I read Delores's first. She said that my old room at the hospital seemed so empty as she sat writing to me. At the end of the letter, Delores wrote, "Even though you didn't ask me to wait, I'll be here when you get back."

Maye poured out her heart and soul in her letter and in all of the later ones she sent. That feeling of premonition was always there, but when I spoke to her on the phone, we would talk until my money ran out, and then I would feel like a hypocrite for doubting her.

Soon I would be eligible for another thirty-day leave. I daydreamed about seeing Maye, the flaming redhead, and Delores, with the movie-star qualities. *How lucky can I get?* I asked myself.

A female sergeant tapped me on the shoulder. "You must be dreaming of home." She needed a ride to the post exchange, and I was the only one with a government driver's license. "What's her name?" she asked.

"Maye and Delores," I sighed.

"You must be a Don Juan."

"Full-blooded Indian," I told her.

"No more questions," she said.

———

In late May I was summoned to the Red Cross office on the base. "You had better make it fast!" the guard told me. So I ran all the way there. Out of breath, I entered the office. I approached a lady seated at a desk. "Corporal Kaquatosh, reporting as ordered."

"Your sister died," the lady said.

"Which one?" I asked.

"Catherine."

"Can't be! I just got a letter from her today."

"You don't understand. Your sister is dead," she said. "I'll get you top priority on the next flight out of Bakersfield. I have a car waiting to take you there."

The driver had my emergency furlough papers with him. He handed them to me.

We just made it to the plane on time. In St. Louis, a general bumped me from my flight, and I had to pay for my own flight to Chicago. From there I had just enough money to take a bus to Wausau. I didn't arrive until early the next morning. I called Maye at the hotel to tell her what had happened.

"I haven't slept since yesterday," I told her.

"Come to the hotel. I'll have a room for you," Maye replied.

When I checked in, I could hardly keep my eyes open. I asked Maye to call me at noon.

When she called me, just before noon, she said, "Ray, if your sister is being buried today, you missed the funeral. Catholics bury only in the morning."

"Well, I have to go home anyway," I said.

Maye was right. They had buried my sister in the morning and wouldn't wait for anyone. Now I had to accept that and grieve with my family. No wonder Catherine had kissed me goodbye when I had left that winter. Now she was dead at the tender age of nineteen. I thought of all of the happy times we had shared, all the fun we had in the summers. Tears flowed from my eyes.

Why do some have to die so young? Why can't the Great Spirit let them live a little longer? What had I done to offend him? *It must be the evil life I've been leading. Maybe what I did overseas?* I wondered. But the nun at St. Mary's had said that would be forgiven. She wouldn't lie.

My mother greeted me with tears of sadness while my wolf stood by my side. He knew what I was going through. "He knows she's gone," my mother said.

"Now I have to go back to the war," I told her.

"Tell him that! He'll understand," she said.

With my youngest sister gone, my mother and my wolf were all that were left for me here. I had to leave this place. On bended knee, I put my arm around my wolf. "Take care of my mother. I'll be back when the war is over. Then we can go fishing and hunting," I promised. He wagged his tail and looked up at me as if to say, *I understand.*

49

Dear John

For the next six weeks back in California, I received letters from Maye. In them she always told me she loved me and couldn't wait until I got back home.

Then I learned I was on the list to go back overseas. With this hanging over my head, I had to use my leave while I had the chance. I was granted leave and made plans to go back to Wausau in two weeks.

Meanwhile, a week passed without any letters from Maye. Finally, just before my leave, the mail clerk handed me a letter. "Is this what you've been waiting for?" I should have said no.

> Dear Ray,
> This is the hardest letter I ever had to write in my whole life. Ray, I'm married…

My premonition had finally come true.

Without reading the rest, I tore it up and threw it in the trash. Many times I have kicked myself for not reading all of it.

My leave time was shortened by the war demands, but while I was in Wausau I was able to spend some time with Delores. The first time we saw each other, she asked, "Is Maye out of your life?"

"Yes," I answered.

"I can't say that I'm sorry."

"When this war is over, I'm coming back to you, and we'll spend all our time making each other happy. I promise."

"You're making me happy now," she said, adding, "and you'll never get a Dear John letter from me."

———

The atomic bomb was dropped on Japan on August 6, 1945. Soon the war would be over. My enlistment orders read: "For the duration of the war and six months." I called Delores and told her I'd be coming home soon.

I had saved all the money from my last furlough. Now all I had to do was wait for Thanksgiving.

Then Delores's letters stopped coming.

One night I called her, and she sounded different somehow. She asked, "Do you still want to marry me?"

"Not while I'm in the service," I replied.

"How long will it be before you're discharged?"

"Maybe after Christmas. Can you wait?" I asked.

She didn't give me a quick answer, and now I knew something really was wrong. Finally she told me that a young doctor was courting her.

Knowing that the doctor would be a better match for her, I knew I had to break our engagement. I hated to, but that was the only way out. When a few weeks later he asked her to marry him, I told her, "Go for it."

50

April

My adventures with women continued back in L.A. There was a pretty sergeant named Gwen, but that is a story for another time. Still, I must tell you about one extraordinary woman I was lucky enough to meet.

Her name was April, and her sister was engaged to another Marine stationed at El Toro. The day I met them, I walked into the Cap Tap, an L.A. bar. They were sitting in a booth, and some sailors were giving them a hard time.

I walked over and asked the Marine, "Need a little help?"

"Yeah, there are four of them."

"Two for you; two for me," I said.

He smiled and said, "By the way, this is my future wife, June, and her sister, April."

"You have another sister named May?"

"No. That's our mother's name."

I used some of my old fighting skills to knock out one of the sailors.

"That was quick," Dan said.

April asked if I had a girlfriend. "I'm a wolf. A lone wolf," I replied.

"I like wolves," April said.

"Then you'd like mine, and me, too."

"Do you have a wolf?" she asked.

"Yes, he's waiting back on the reservation."

"Got any pictures of him?" she asked.

"Yes, tacked on my locker door."

"Will you bring one for me next time you come to L.A.?"

"Just for you." April's eyes seemed to sparkle like green emeralds. Her red hair enhanced her countenance. Her nose was tiny and turned up like a baby's. When she smiled, I saw that her teeth were pearly white.

Dan and June were getting married the next weekend. He asked, "Can you make it?"

"I'll go over the hill if I have to," I told him.

April put her cheek on mine and whispered, "See ya Saturday."

The days dragged by until Saturday. I was impatient until April met me to go to the Cap Tap. She rushed over to me and said, "Ray, I'm so glad you could make it. Come with me!" She grabbed my hand and pulled me toward the car.

"April . . . that reminds me of spring. You're my kind of woman," I told her.

"Really?" she said, covering a cough.

"I've been dreaming about you all week," I replied.

"I don't know what to say!"

"You believe in love at first sight?" I asked.

"Yes."

"I'm in love with you."

"Have you been drinking?" she asked.

"Haven't had a beer since last week. Will you marry me?" I asked.

"Yes!" she answered quickly.

"You just made me the happiest man in the world."

"If I'm dreaming, don't wake me!" she said.

After we parked, she pulled me all the way in to the Cap Tap. She then pulled me to the booth where Dan and June were sitting and announced, "We're engaged!" Dan looked at June quizzically. Then he said, "Congratulations." June got up and hugged April. She had tears in her eyes.

Dan got up and said to me, "We'll be family now."

"Okay, brother Dan," I said. Then I added, "April, I have $150, and next weekend I'll get you an engagement ring. Then you set the date."

"Do you really mean that?" she said. She coughed again.

Dan looked worried and asked, "Are you okay, April?"

"I feel fine," she replied.

June looked worried and stared at her for a long time. "Sit down and rest a while," she told her.

April sat on my lap. She was light as a feather. Dan looked at me and said, "You better seal that with a kiss."

April stood up and stretched her arms out to me. As I stood waiting, she reached for my face, cupping my face in her hands and gently pulling me down to her lips. They were as soft, warm, and delicate as a butterfly's wings—a velvet touch. She held me like that for a long time. Then she slowly released my face and slipped her arms around my neck. I was enthralled. I tenderly held her close to my chest. I didn't want to release her. She whispered, "Now we're officially engaged."

I turned to face all of the people in the bar and shouted, "I JUST GOT ENGAGED!" Everyone clapped. The bartender hollered, "The next drink is on me!" Dan shook my hand, and June gave me a hug and kissed my cheek.

April coughed again, and June said, "Here, drink some beer."

She reached for me, and I held her in my arms. She was trembling like she was cold. With her head pressed against my chest, she said, "Ray, I'll make you the best wife in the whole world. You're the only man I've ever kissed that way, and I'll never kiss another, for the rest of my life."

I said, "April, I'm getting a seven-day pass tomorrow. Let's get married soon."

"Sure. Just hold me. Never, never let me go."

We left the bar and headed to her place. She stated to cough as we entered the house. "You better knock off the smoking," I said.

"I don't smoke," she answered quickly. I should have known that something was wrong. "Ray, I'm a little tired. I'm going to take a nap. Don't leave me, promise?"

Without saying another word, I lifted her in my arms and slowly walked to the bedroom. I found a blanket to cover her and then stood gazing at this little lady who would soon by my wife. I slipped off my shoes, shirt, and tie and joined her. Lying next to her, I slipped my arm under her neck, and she moved her head on to my chest.

The next day we went to a movie. Many times during the show I glanced down at her, and once in a while she'd stretch up and kiss my cheek. Then I'd whisper, "I'll never wash it off." We went back to the Cap Tap, where we sat in a booth and listened to my favorite song, "Begin the Beguine," performed by Artie Shaw. She said, "I like this song! How did you know that it's my favorite?"

"Really? Now it will be our song."

We got home about midnight, and she changed into a gown that touched the floor.

"Do you know the words to our song?" she asked.

"Yes. I've listened to it many times."

"Repeat them to me," she whispered.

"When they begin the beguine, it brings back a sound of music so tender; it brings back a night of tropical splendor; it brings back a memory evergreen . . ."

"I like the beginning," she said. She floated toward the dining room.

I lay back and pulled a blanket over my chest and settled down for sleep. I felt a gentle tap on my shoulder. She reached out her arms to me, and I thought she wanted a goodnight kiss. So I stood up, and she pulled me toward the bedroom. Without saying a word, she pulled back the covers, crawled in, and sat waiting for me to join her. She said, "Ray, if we're going to be man and wife, we'd better start now. We haven't much time." I thought she was referring to June and Dan coming back early, but we had all night.

Later, I wondered if I should have waited until we were married. But then I saw April's smiling face. She sighed, "Mrs. April Kaquatosh. I'll be Mrs. April Kaquatosh." She brushed her cheek against mine and asked, "What are the other words to our song?"

"I'm with you once more under the stars, and down by the shore the orchestra's playing, and even the palms seem to be swaying, when they begin the beguine. To live it again is past all endeavor, except when that tune clutches my heart, and there we are, swearing to love forever, and promising never, never to part . . ."

"Ray, we'll love forever, and we'll promise never to part."

It was a wonderful moment, one I will never forget, but when she got up, she coughed again. I thought it must be the start of a cold. I asked her if there was anything I could do for her. "No, I've been having these periods of coughing and shortness of breath. Also, I feel weak."

"Have you consulted a doctor?" I asked.

"Yes, they took some tests last week, and I have to return to the hospital on Monday." Then she added, "I was in a sanitarium for a while. Forgive me. I should have told you."

"No need to apologize. I was sick with malaria last January."

"Ray, I feel tired again."

"Get to bed. I'll wake you when Dan gets here."

Her cough was becoming more frequent. Still, she fell asleep. The phone rang, and I jumped to pick it up. It was Dan. "Dan, get here fast! April is sick."

"We should have told you."

When Dan got back he said, "Ray, I have a confession to make. We didn't think you'd ask her to marry you, and we didn't think she'd accept. She has to go to the sanitarium tomorrow. She has lung disease."

"How long will she be there?" I asked.

"We don't know yet."

"Then I'm taking part of my leave, starting tomorrow."

"You really love her, don't you?" he asked.

"More than any woman in my whole life," I told him.

———

Later Dan drove around to the front and honked the horn. As April started to walk toward the car, she lost her balance. I picked her up and carried her to the car.

On the way to the hospital, June started to cry. April smiled and held my hand all the way to the hospital. I tried to comfort her, and she fell asleep.

When we arrived, I picked her up again and carried her to the entrance. The nurses had a wheelchair waiting. I gently placed her body down, and she gave my hand a slight squeeze. The nurses rushed her into the isolation ward, where they placed her in an oxygen tent. She smiled and waved to me. Then a nurse said, "Put on that mask!"

I held her hand until she fell asleep. She looked so peaceful.

"Keep me informed. I have to return to the base," I told Dan as I left.

"Ray, thank you for everything," said June. "There's nothing we can do for her now," she added.

Coming face to face with this reality made me angry about all the beliefs of a nurturing supreme being. How could the Great Spirit let this happen? Staring into the psychological abyss was overwhelming, leaving me unable to function.

The next day, I asked for two days off, and my request was approved. I returned to the hospital. April smiled as I entered her room.

I had brought with me the picture of my wolf, and I handed it to her.

"Beautiful! Tell me about him."

"He's about eleven years old. He sleeps out in the snow all winter. When he gets hungry, he goes hunting for his supper. Loves women, and he's waiting for you."

"I want to see him!" She stood the picture up near her head. "Ray, I'm feeling a little better. Don't leave me."

"I have two days off. I'll be right here." She breathed a sigh of relief and asked for more words to our song.

"What moments divine, what rapture serene, till clouds came along to disperse the joys we had tasted; and now when I hear people curse the chance that was wasted, I know but too well what they mean, so don't let them begin the beguine . . ."

"That's the best part. I'll always love you." She dozed off. I left a note telling her I'd be back soon.

It was the beginning of the end, and I knew it. This compelled me to seek refuge in common traditional activities, spiritual practices, and rituals. I knew I must accept the Great Spirit's wisdom. I could not go backward, only forward, knowing that chaos will always happen when I least expect it.

For weeks I returned to the hospital, until April could no longer recognize me. Dan said, "Ray, if it's any comfort to you, she asked about you on several occasions, but she was too weak to open her eyes. We always told her you were waiting."

She became comatose not long after one of my visits. After that, I never went back.

One day Dan told me the bad news. She was gone. But how could I ever forget April? She will always be in my dreams, and our song will always be "'Begin the Beguine." I hope the Great Spirit permits me to see her again in the Happy Hunting Ground.

April was buried with the picture of my wolf by her side.

51

Home Once More

In the spring of 1946, after three years in the Marines, I was discharged. I could hear my wolf calling. It was time to go back home.

But when I got there, my wolf wasn't around—probably out hunting rabbits. He was free to go anytime he wanted to. That's the way of the wolf. He had to be free, just like me.

My mother was in her forties. Her long hair, which she always wore curled into a knot on the back of her head, still had no gray. "Have you given thanks to the Great Spirit for your safe return?" she asked me.

"No, but I will right now."

Soon my wolf scratched on the door, and I slowly opened it. He didn't enter. He just stood there looking at me. I said, "Kernel, don't you remember me?" He twisted his head, sniffed the air, and then that old bushy tail started to wag. He jumped on my arm and licked my hand. Then he bolted to the door. He stopped and turned to me as if to say, *Let's go hunting!*

"He's been waiting a long time for this moment," my mother said. "You better take him for a long walk and talk to him. Remember, he understands what you say." She was right.

We walked along the Wolf River, watching the redwing blackbirds building their nests and a loon paddling along. We heard the crows cawing at each other, saw a gopher scurry across the road, watched a squirrel jump from branch to branch, and felt the warm spring breeze.

My old fishing hole hadn't changed. None of these places changed. Only people changed. I knew I would never return here and live like I used to. I had grown up, and I had changed. Sitting on the riverbank with my arm around my wolf, I said to him, "Kernel, I have to leave you again. I'll return from time to time during the summer. When our last breath is taken, we'll be together forever. It's only a matter of time." He just looked at the ground. I knew he understood.

I'll always remember him like that, with his thick fur and bushy tail, offering me his paw.

We walked on. Kernel sniffed the air and the ground. He ran ahead of me, turned around, and run back with his tail wagging. He went looking for game. "Don't go too far!" I told him. He stopped and looked at me, then ran toward the pines. A little while later I called for him, and he came running. "Look, we got enough for supper," I showed him my catch. He wagged his tail as if to acknowledge that we did indeed have enough.

When we got back to the house, my mother said, "I was about to come looking for you."

"You never have to worry when Kernel is with me," I told her.

My mother made fried bread and fried the trout with potatoes and onions. We each had two trout. Kernel licked his chops, then wagged his tail and gave me a paw. "He's saying thanks for his favorite dish," my mother said.

———

All that summer Kernel and I went hunting and fishing. One day he caught a rabbit, dropped it at my feet, and wagged his tail until I picked it up. We returned home, and my mother cooked it. We gave him most of it. Every time I left, I'd reach down for his paw, he'd lift one, I'd scratch it, pet his head, and turn to walk to the car. He wouldn't follow me. He knew I was leaving.

The summer passed too quickly, and although I had just turned twenty-two, I had to return to Wausau to finish high school. I visited home during the cool weather, taking Kernel rabbit hunting around Thanksgiving time, but with my studies I had time for only a few visits until the snow came.

In winter my wolf's coat would turn white. He never ate sweets; he was a meat-and-potatoes eater just like me. He even tried to drink some beer once, but the bubbles made him sneeze. He never went to a vet, even the time he was shot. Whenever he got a sliver in his paw, he would limp to me and wait for me to remove it. Then he'd lick my hand to say thanks.

My wolf didn't show signs of aging like dogs do. But old Father Time waits for no one. We're here today and gone tomorrow.

52

The One and Only

I moved back to Wausau to attend high school, for which the military paid me sixty-five dollars a month. One day I stepped on the bus to go to the hospital. As I sat down, I saw a petite young blonde sitting farther back on the bus. She didn't seem to notice me, so I edged toward the back to get a better look as I passed by her. She continued to look forward. When the bus got to Humboldt Avenue, she stepped off. As she walked east on Humboldt, I got a view of her profile. I was captivated.

After she got off, I asked the bus driver, "Who was the movie star that just got off?"

"I don't know, but she takes this bus frequently from downtown at 5:15."

"See ya at 5:15 tomorrow," I told him. He just laughed.

Later, at the Forest Bar, my friend Irene Freidl, the owner, said, "You look like you're ready for the loony bin." She set my beer down. "Tell Ma about her!"

We laughed and shook the dice to see who would put a quarter in the jukebox. "It's no use. I'll never see her again," I moaned.

"Blonde or brunette?"

"Sort of a honey blonde."

Irene smiled and said, "I know, you'd like to have her as your honey." We had a good laugh at that one.

When the weekend came around, my friend Don said, "How 'bout a few beers tonight?"

"Sounds good, but I'm kinda broke," I told him.

"My sister will lend me a few dollars," he said.

"Okay, see ya at Braatz's Bar about nine."

Beer was ten cents a glass, the juke played six songs for a quarter, and the pinball machine was five cents. Two dollars lasted a long time, and we got tipsy before too long. On the way home that night, I almost stepped in front of a moving car as it turned the corner in front of me. *Gotta get that gal out of my mind,* I thought. But try as I might, I couldn't.

Payday came on the first of every month. In between, I was always pretty broke. This month was no exception. Don was aware of this, and one day he asked, "Can you make it over to my home for supper?"

"Anytime you say. I'll be there," I said.

"Meet me at Braatz's at six."

The Great Spirit smiled on me that day. After we had a quick beer, we walked the short distance to Don's house, which was on Humboldt Avenue. Don opened the door and said, "Mom, this is Ray."

"Hi, Ray. I'm Hazel," Don's mother said.

A young blonde woman entered the room, and Don said, "Ray, this is my sister, Elaine."

She was the same girl who had eluded me on the bus. For a few seconds, I was mesmerized by her smile. She held me spellbound without even trying.

"Hi, Elaine."

"Hi, Ray."

I couldn't believe what was happening. I thought I must be dreaming, and if I was, I hoped it would last a little longer. Finally I managed to say, "Thanks for inviting me over for supper."

"You're welcome any time, Ray," Hazel smiled.

"Ray was in the Marines during the war," said Don.

"Welcome back," said Elaine. She was about two years younger than me. Her smile intrigued me. For the first time in my life, I forgot about checking a young woman's vital statistics.

After supper Don and I walked over to his favorite watering hole and lifted a few. "What do you think of my sister?" he asked.

I couldn't let on what I really thought of her. "Really nice," I said. Then I had a thought. "Maybe we can all go out for a fish fry on Friday. I just got paid!"

Don liked the idea. "Sounds good to me," he said.

On the walk home, I couldn't stop thinking about Elaine. In fact, I couldn't stop thinking of her all the next day. I was in love. Maybe it was all in vain. Or maybe she'd go out for that fish fry on Friday. I'd have a talk with my Creator and ask for help.

After classes, I often walked over to the Forest Bar and chatted with Irene and with her friend Mary, a pretty brunette who was visiting from up north in Boulder Junction. Irene always asked if I had my homework done. Then they asked if I had seen the blonde. I kept telling them, "I won't until Friday."

One afternoon, Mary said, "Ray, if she turns you down, I'll buy you the best fish fry in town."

"I think you'll be buying. I haven't heard from her brother."

On Friday afternoon when I met up with Don, I knew from

the expression on his face that our fish fry date was off. "Ray, I tried," he said, "but my mother wants to go out for a fish fry. But we can meet after dinner at Braatz's."

"I'll be there," I smiled, "with bells on." On the way back to the bar, I kicked at stones, jumped at the low-hanging branches, whirled around, and skipped like a kid. I felt really happy for the first time since I'd had to say good-bye to April.

Around six o'clock I walked over to my watering hole. When I entered, I told Irene that I'd gotten all my homework done. She laughed and told me that I could now have my beer.

"What about your fish fry?" asked Mary, sitting a few stools down from me.

"She couldn't make it, but I'll be meeting her in two hours and ten minutes—no, make that two hours and nine minutes."

"Then what?"

"I don't know. I'm scared. I wish I was back in the war. Maybe she doesn't like Indians," I answered.

"Damn it!" scoffed Mary. "If she's that way, I'll take you back to Boulder Junction and be proud of you."

I think she really meant it. "Mary," I said, "I'd like to buy you a fish fry."

After supper, Mary and I headed back to the Forest Bar. We had a few beers and listened to the jukebox, and then Irene reminded me that it was time to meet Don and Elaine. "Get your butt over there and ask her out!" she said.

While I was walking over to meet them, I did a lot of thinking. I was sure my prospects were dim. I decided that after tonight I would return to L.A. But how would I forget about Elaine in L.A. if I couldn't forget about her in Wausau?

All my negative thoughts disappeared when I approached the booth where Elaine and her friend Betty were waiting for me. Elaine's radiant disposition banished all my worries. She had me spellbound again. Just watching her smile made me happy. I thought, *I'll never go back to L.A. now.*

Don came over and handed me a glass of beer, saying, "We were worried. We thought you couldn't make it."

I laughed, "Wild horses couldn't hold me back when you're buying!" Soon we were having such a nice time that I almost forgot about asking Elaine for a date. But I managed to suggest seeing a movie at the Grand Theatre and, to my surprise, Elaine accepted. Only one thing was wrong. I had said it in front of Betty, and she wanted to go along. I informed her that I could afford to take only one person with me. Betty assured me that she could pay her own way. "Is that okay with you, Ray?"

"Sure," I answered. "The more the merrier."

As they left, Elaine said, "Nice meeting you again." I almost flipped. I reached out to shake her hand, and she obliged. If my battery had been dead, it was now fully charged.

I turned to Don and asked, "Got time for a nightcap?" He did.

"Good," I said. "Put in a good word for me with your sister."

Don got wise. "For a beer, I'll do it."

"Have two," I offered, and we smiled and clinked our glasses.

On the way home, I damn near got hit by a tree. Funny thing about trees, they stand stationary, but once in a while they jump right out in front of you. Then a curb kicked me and I fell on my ass. Who cares? I was flying without wings. It must have been something in the beer.

53

Destiny

Elaine and I had no control over our destiny. We were mere mortals struggling toward our predetermined fate. Long before I saw Elaine on the bus, she had observed me walking on the street. She told a girlfriend, "Someday I'm going to marry that man."

She had yearned to meet me. She later told me that her anguish was identical to mine after I had my first glimpse of her. When she revealed all this to me, I couldn't believe it. I was grateful for all the blessings the Great Spirit provided for us. I knew he had chosen Elaine to fill the void in my life. The Great Spirit had sent me a wolf; now he had sent me a mate.

When we met at the Grand Theatre, I offered Elaine my arm. Then I noticed the sad expression on Betty's face, so I offered her my other arm, and her face lit up. But even the extra company on our date could not deter us. The movie seemed immaterial. Holding Elaine's hand was more important. Sitting next to her was exhilarating. That night Elaine and I started a never-ending love. From that day on she was my one and only, and she remains so to this day.

Our romance began early in the spring of 1947. We made all the stops around Wausau: theaters, fairs, the Dells of the Eau Claire River, Rib Mountain, and the outdoor movies. Because of the feelings I harbored about my stepfather and brothers, I did not take her to the reservation to meet my wolf. Yet Elaine never complained. She seemed to understand why I wanted to stay away from them.

———

The North Wind had bowed to the South Wind, and the summer breeze was soft. The earth had turned green. This is the time when everything blossoms, including romance.

Our first summer together was the happiest I've ever had. We had each other, and no one else mattered. Sometimes our friend Betty would get annoyed when she noticed us holding hands. But we were discreet and never displayed passionate affections in public.

Elaine was a devout Catholic, and she didn't frequent bars. The only one she patronized was Braatz's, which was a family bar. When I invited her to the Forest Bar, she declined. I was content just to have the privilege of escorting her to the theater, restaurants, and social events.

One day Irene asked me, "How's your blonde?"

"Fine. She works just a couple blocks from here."

"When are you going to bring her in?"

"She doesn't go to bars," I told her.

"The lady has class," Irene said.

"Her mother also maintains those standards."

"They appear to have an ethical and virtuous social status," Irene replied.

"Yes, contrary to my inveterate propensity to consume the brew," I said.

"Have you been reading the dictionary again?" she asked.

"Yes, I've been trying to figure out why I have this habitual inclination to sit here and consume this so called 'nectar-of-the-gods,'" I said.

"You don't need a dictionary for that. You just like my company."

Most of my leisure time was spent at the Forest Bar, and if I didn't report in, Irene would become worried. She was concerned about my welfare. Being an Indian in a "white man's world," I was at a disadvantage.

While attending high school in Wausau, I met a young man who was eager to hear about my wartime experiences. He had heard that I was shot during the war. I told him I was trying to forget about it. "Stop in Rudy's Wonder Bar; my father owns it," he pressed.

When I entered the bar, it was packed with people, and I had to wait. The bartender took his time. Finally he approached me at the same time my friend walked up to me. "I can't serve you," the bartender said.

"Here's my driver's license. I'm twenty-two years old."

"I can't serve you because you're an Indian," he yelled.

"What?" exclaimed my classmate. "You can't treat a wounded veteran like that!" Some of the patrons started to walk out. My friend followed me out the door and stopped me on the steps to apologize for what the bartender had said. "Wait until my father hears about this."

The people who walked out with me shook my hand. One of them said, "I own a tavern just outside the city. Come and see us, I'd like to buy you one."

When Rudy heard about what happened, he fired the bartender. My friend said, "You're welcome here anytime."

Sometime later, I walked into a tavern on the west side of town. I sat down and was about to order when I saw that the same bartender who had refused to serve me was now working there. I turned to walk out.

"Wait! Come back! I'd like to buy you one," he called after me. "Forgive me for being so stupid."

Prejudice is not uncommon in our society. It's prevalent among the lower social stratification—or should I say, the uneducated, the misinformed, the ignorant. Some of Elaine's relatives thought she should not associate with an Indian, which infuriated her. She defied their remarks, their ridicule, and the scornful attitudes toward my Indian heritage.

I knew the Great Spirit had chosen her for me, and therefore no one could stand in the way of our destiny.

54

Wings

Since I first saw the hawk soaring effortlessly above the Wolf River when I was about to become a man, I knew I had to fly. After all, am I not the Little Hawk?

One day Elaine surprised me by saying, "Let's go to the airport."

As we approached the hangar, I saw a large sign: FLIGHT SCHOOL, INQUIRE HERE. I said, "Elaine, I'm going to start training to become a pilot."

"Really?" she beamed.

Flight instructor Lyle Grimm was standing at the front desk. "Can I help you?" he asked.

"Yes, I'd like to sign up for flight school."

"Okay. Fill out these papers."

Elaine was so happy she squeezed my arm and bounced up and down. She asked, "When do you start?"

"Ground school starts tomorrow for six weeks, then I start flying."

Ground school taught me many things I would need to know to be a pilot: navigation, traffic rules, radio, meteorology, using aerodynamics instruments. I did well in all the courses.

One day Lyle took us out to where the planes were parked and said, "This is an airplane."

Someone said, "I thought it was a yellow cab."

"Quiet back there!" hollered Lyle. "Who wants to be the first to go up?"

When I was in the Marines, I had learned to never volunteer. Some other guy stepped forward, and he and Lyle took off, circled the field, and landed. When the plane stopped, Lyle got out and helped the student out of the plane. He puked all over himself and part of the plane, too. One of the other students said, "I'm not going up in that plane."

Lyle turned and asked, "Ray, you wanna go up?"

"Sure," I said, "after you clean up the back seat."

"We'll use another plane," he said.

"Let's go!" I replied. We taxied out to the landing strip and checked the left magneto, then the right. Now we were ready for takeoff. We looked for planes landing and none were in sight, so we gave the plane full throttle and started rolling down the runway. Soon we were airborne.

We reached the altitude of 1,500 feet, and Lyle said, "See that barn? Fly us over there!" Straight and level flight. I did it!

"Take us back to the field," said Lyle. "Keep the nose up! You're doing fine."

When we landed, I hollered over and over: "I flew it!" Then I noticed the sad face of the guy who had gotten sick. I walked over to him and said, "Feeling any better?"

"I'll never make it," he said.

"Next time, don't eat a heavy meal before takeoff!" I replied.

He looked surprised and said, "I had a malted milk."

"You don't have it anymore," I replied.

After all the other students had their first lesson, I took the sad fellow over to Lyle and said, "He'd like to try again."

"Think he's ready?" asked Lyle.

"Sure, just give him another chance."

"Let's go."

The guy looked worried, so I gave him a little encouragement. "You don't have a full stomach now, so you can't get sick. Show these guys you can do it!"

"I'll try."

A half hour later they landed, and the man jumped out of the plane, ran over to me, and said, "Ray, I did it!" He gave me a bear hug and laughed.

Now the fun really began. In each lesson, we performed different maneuvers: steep turns, stalls, and most exciting, tailspins.

After twenty-five hours of flight instruction, I was ready for my first solo flight. As Elaine stood near the fence to watch, Lyle said, "Take off and circle the field. Then bring it in for a landing." As I took off, I could see Elaine waving at me. She seemed no bigger than a postage stamp.

My first solo flight ended with a lot of handshakes and back-slapping from all of the ground crew, my instructors, and Lyle's wife, Marie. Elaine was all smiles as I hugged her.

Now that I was a fledgling, I had to exercise my wings. This would take twenty hours of solo flights before I could qualify for my pilot's certificate. I had a dual cross-country flight and a solo cross-country flight coming up. Then I had to be checked out by the Federal Aviation Administration to verify that I qualified to be a pilot.

I made it. The FAA issued me a temporary pilot's permit, meaning I could fly solo. Then I received my official certificate in the mail. My number is 1001675. I was the first or second

Menominee Indian from the reservation to hold a pilot's certificate. Lyle later told me I was the only Indian to earn a pilot's certificate at his airport.

Now that I had earned my wings, I was no longer considered the Little Hawk. I would be referred to as the Hawk. My mother would be proud of me. She knew I had always wanted to fly like a hawk.

55

Hawk's Mate

By the summer of 1947 I had decided to commit fully to our relationship. Elaine seemed to sense this and suggested we go for a walk in the park by the railroad tracks.

I proposed on bended knee. "Will you marry me?" I asked.

She smiled and shouted yes, throwing her arms around my neck and sealing it with a kiss.

Soon I started attending school in Stevens Point. But being separated from Elaine was more than I could endure. She was on my mind constantly. I returned to Wausau and took a job at Maas' Service Station. And we planned our wedding.

We contracted a Catholic priest in Wausau and asked if he would perform the ceremony. He flatly refused because of my Indian heritage. It was like being kicked in the stomach by a mule.

Prejudice from a Catholic priest? I couldn't believe it. Elaine was shocked and almost in tears. It took a while to regain our composure. "There are other priests," she said. Two others refused. I began to hate priests. What fools these mortals were to attempt to deter a divine power! No mere mortal could prevent our destiny.

"I'll never go back to church," I said.

Elaine showed her wisdom when she said, "Don't condemn the Catholic Church for what a few priests did!" That remark reminded me of something I had learned when I studied religion. When Christ was nailed to the cross and was dying, he said, "Forgive them, Father, for they know not what they do." If he could forgive his tormenters, who was I to hold a grudge?

With this new outlook, I was determined to seek out another priest to perform the ceremony. Finally we found one. He was reluctant, and he would not allow us to go to the altar of his church to give thanks to the Almighty. But who cares? We were married, and that was all that mattered to us. May the Great Spirit forgive him for his futile attempt to prevent a match made in heaven.

As we scurried out of the rectory toward wedded bliss, I boasted, "You are Mrs. Raymond C. Kaquatosh!" We were the happiest people on earth.

———

It was late autumn, and the leaves had fallen. It was time for me to make an offering of thanks to the Great Spirit for sending me my one and only.

Don lent me his car so I could return to the reservation. My wolf was waiting. He wagged his tail as I approached, letting me know he hadn't forgotten me. His coat was turning white for the coming winter.

My mother said, "He knew you were coming. He got restless about an hour ago." That was about the time I had left Wausau. "Tell him what's been happening in your life," she urged.

"Should I tell him I got married?"

"Yes, he'll understand," she told me.

He always bowed his head when I talked to him, his way of listening. I believe he understood everything.

EPILOGUE

After our wedding, Elaine and I moved to southern Wisconsin, where work was more plentiful. We settled in Beloit, where over time I had jobs in a restaurant, at Fairbanks Morse Engine making locomotives, at a foundry, and as a route salesman for the Omar Baking Company. Soon we were settled in our first home and had all our furniture paid for, money in the bank, and a car to drive. Of course, it was the calm before the storm.

In autumn 1950 a letter arrived from Washington, D.C. All Marine Reserves were being called to active duty for the Korean War. I was put on twenty-four-hour notice.

Soon I got my orders to report to a Marine base in North Carolina, and Elaine went to stay with her mother in Wausau. But less than a year later, on August 2, 1951, I was discharged, having seen no action in Korea.

As I boarded the train to Milwaukee, I thought of my wolf. My mother had written to me every month, reporting his condition. In her last letter, she had said he was losing his eyesight. I had to hurry home. Maybe I could take him to a vet. But I knew he would never let anyone else handle him.

I drove to the reservation. When I went into the house, Kernel was asleep, and my mother cautioned me to be quiet. He was resting comfortably, and she didn't want to wake him. Mother and I talked for a long time. As we did, I kept looking at the wonderful animal that had shared my childhood.

He was sleeping most of the day and was almost blind. His hearing was going as well. Nevertheless, he sensed I was there. He tried to wag his tail and limped toward the door. As I opened it for him, he slowly walked out, and I said these words: "Kernel, you are an old man now. One of these days . . ."

"Don't talk to him like that!" my mother admonished me. She was crying, something she rarely did. I knew I had offended my wolf. "He saw you through two wars, and now his job is done," she said, still crying.

After hours of calling for him, I gave up and returned to the house. I couldn't face my mother with tears in my eyes. The next day, I searched far and wide again, but still I couldn't find him. "When the North Wind howls, you'll know it's him," my mother said.

She later wrote to tell me Kernel did not return. She said I would never see him again.

But I know it's only a matter of time. Sometimes I dream of him. I know he waits in the Happy Hunting Ground to show me around.

ACKNOWLEDGMENTS

My sincere gratitude to my grandson Ian and to Michael J. Marinoff for their unselfish contributions and assistance in making this book possible.

Special thanks to my dear wife, Elaine M. Kaquatosh, for her assistance in remembering our early acquaintance.

Last, I wish to express my profound thanks to the following friends:

Frank J. Balistreri, Jr.	Aimee Lepscier
Diane Cairney	Alex Lepscier
Robert Cairney	Dawn Lepscier
Ben and Irene Freidl	Mary Lepscier
Frances Friedl	Richard Lepscier
James B. Freidl	Kay Neumer
Mary Ann Freidl	Larry Richter
James Henderson	Roberta Oshkosh Robinson
Jenny Henderson	Margaret Snow
Karla Kitson	Yvette Snow
Larry W. Kies	

We cannot live in the past or the future. We must accept life as it is and never complain about trivial things. There is so much to do and so little time. When my last breath is taken, I will be with my wolf again. Then we will be at peace forever and roam the heavens for all eternity.

Hope the Great Spirit smiles on us from time to time.

Raymond C. Kaquatosh, January 1945

ABOUT THE AUTHOR

Raymond Claud Kaquatosh was born in 1924 in Neopit, Wisconsin. He spent his early years on the Menominee Indian Reservation and at the Menominee Boarding School at Keshena. Ray served in the US Marine Corps in World War II and the Korean War and later attended high schools in Keshena, Wausau, and Stevens Point; Milwaukee Area Technical College; the University of Wisconsin–Milwaukee; and the University of Wisconsin Law School. In August 1947 he became one of the first Menominee Indians to earn a pilot's certificate. He walked on in 2018 at age ninety-three.